LIBRARY OF LATIN AMERICAN
HISTORY AND CULTURE

GENERAL EDITOR:
DR. A. CURTIS WILGUS

INTER-AMERICAN BIBLIOGRAPHICAL
and
LIBRARY ASSOCIATION
PUBLICATIONS

SERIES I, VOLUME 9

Makers of Democracy in Latin America

BY

HAROLD E. DAVIS
Professor of History
The American University
Washington, D. C.

COOPER SQUARE PUBLISHERS, INC.
NEW YORK   1968

Copyright © 1945 by Harold E. Davis
New Introduction Copyright © 1968 by Harold E. Davis
Published by Cooper Square Publishers, Inc.
59 Fourth Avenue, New York, N. Y. 10003
Library of Congress Catalog Card No. 68-56190

Printed in the United States of America
by Sentry Press, New York, N. Y. 10019

PREFACE

By extending the privilege of a new Preface in this reprint of a work written a quarter of a century ago, Cooper Square Publishers have given the author a chance to reappraise some of his ideas. He has also been given an opportunity to acknowledge again some old debts for assistance and encouragement. Paul Bellamy, then editor of the *Cleveland Plain Dealer*, opened the columns of his paper in 1941-42 to some of the sketches which make up this book; the editors of *World Affairs*, the organ of the century-and-a-half old American Peace Society, published in June 1944 the author's article, "Democracy in Latin America," which expressed some of the seminal ideas of the present work; A. Curtis Wilgus was then editor of *World Affairs;* he also joined in sponsoring the *Makers of Democracy in Latin America* by giving it a place in a series of publications of the Inter-American Bibliographical and Library Association. To all, my thanks.

Some of the biographies might be written differently today, in the light of more recent scholarship. New titles would certainly appear in the select bibliographies. But the general interpretations would not change. It is my belief now, as then, that a better understanding of the peoples of what we call Latin America is furthered by the knowledge that they have produced leaders with the courage of their convictions, whether in success or failure. This new edition does not permit rewriting of the text. But even if it did, I would not want to change what I then wrote in any substantial respect. For the book was an expression of the growing concern of the years of World War II for the prospect of a democratic Latin America. It seemed important then to see that the concepts of democracy to which these Latin American leaders had sought to give form and direction were none the less real merely because they differed from those of North America. So I defined democracy, in the Introduction, as "the American spirit in Latin America, the essence of its struggles for independence, the liberation of Negro slaves, its gradual assimilation of the Indian population, and its fundamental belief in the attainment of a better order of society and better life through fuller participation of the masses of men and women in its making." The stereotyped caricatures of Latin American political leaders to which readers of the nineteen forties had been accustomed made it important to urge this historical and sociological view of democracy. The reality of the democratic commitment of Latin America needed to be understood as the aspiration of a people conditioned by their historical experiences and their cultural values, rather than as any specific political system. Today, I would like to believe, this view would be accepted without much question by intelligent readers.

Chevy Chase, Maryland
July 8, 1968

H.E.D.

CONTENTS

INTRODUCTION

DEMOCRACY IN LATIN AMERICA

Our age, possibly more than any other, is devoted to historical and biographical literature. In particular, the lives of past and present leaders of democracy fill the pages of our books, our newspapers and our magazines. Yet somehow, in this instance as in others, we have tended to overlook Latin America. Although the history of our southern neighbor republics touches ours in many ways, and reveals scores of writers, artists, scientists, and political and social leaders who have given themselves unstintingly, and often at great sacrifice and risk, to the tasks of forming prosperous democratic societies, we in the United States know little of these leaders. This volume will deal only with those who have labored at the political and social aspects of building democratic societies and governments. A complete hall of fame would include many more, not only in the social and political fields, but in such fields as literature, art, music, religion and science as well.

Behind the pageantry of revolutions, of self-seeking politicians, of militarists and self-conscious dictators strutting their brief moments of unenviable distinction on the stage of their countries' history, lies the real Latin America. It is a Latin America which varies widely in democratic achievement from country to country, and which frequently presents the widest range of difference in social and economic achievement within a given country. It consists of millions of hardworking, humble folk, restless and confused by their own destiny. It is a dynamic, expanding society, wrestling with its mountains, struggling in the conquest of its vast plains and its tropical river valleys, and of its rich natural resources. It is a new society, with a new and rapidly growing population, rising slowly out of the Indian, European and Negro populations and the diverse cultural elements which have gone into its making. Gifted in many ways, but frustrated and sometimes exploited, it is a society bursting its bonds of tradition and colonial dependence, assimilating the new ways of a technological and industrial order, and frequently revolting against it. But above all it is dynamic, growing, expanding, with its eyes on the future. For those who have eyes to see, it is calling clearly for political, technical, cultural and spiritual leadership of the highest order of skill, insight and determination, to organize its growing activity and power. This need for leadership is great and always has been great. Leaders of first rank have appeared all too infrequently. Yet, as the succeeding pages will show, there are many Latin Americans who have played outstanding parts in the American epic struggle for democracy.

To understand this leadership properly it is necessary to have some understanding of the elements of democracy in Latin America, the elements to which the leadership has attempted to give form, purpose and direction. Although it is difficult for North Americans to understand, Latin America has a democracy which is none the less real for being different in many respects from its North American cousin. It varies widely in degree of development from backward Honduras to advanced Uruguay, Chile or Mexico. It also varies considerably from time to time within a given country. But it continues its irresistible growth irrespective of political vicissitudes. Democracy is the American spirit in Latin America, the essence of its struggles for independence, its liberation of Negro slaves, its gradual assimilation of the Indian population, and its fundamental belief in the attainment of a better order of society and better life through fuller and freer participation of the masses of men and women in its making.

Democracy, like dictatorship, is not an absolute, alike wherever encountered. It exists in many different forms and degrees. It is a fact of history, not a proposition of theology. It is a characteristic of certain patterns of political behavior infused with strong spiritual elements, the essence of which is this belief in the attainment of a better economic and social order through fuller equality of opportunity and freer participation of ordinary men and women in the political process.

Democracy in Latin America is to be seen, therefore, in the individual's sense of this freedom and equality, in each country's devotion to its independence, in a highly developed sense of human dignity, and in the persistent search for the good society. It is to be seen particularly in the persistence of its leaders in that search even when the difficulties have appeared insurmountable. In these qualities Latin America abounds, as in the enthusiasm and optimism which we have come to identify as American, and to think of as a product of New World pioneering.

In an even more fundamental sense democracy is to be seen in our southern neighbors in the steady tendency revealed in their history to broaden the basis of society and the state, and to break down the class and race distinctions originating long ago in the European conquest, or even before. In some of the republics one can see that the stress and turmoil of political life has been closely connected with the rise to political power of the mestizo class.[1] In Mexico, for example, this was apparently the basic socio-political development of the nineteenth century. The instability of Mexican political life was thus an outward manifestation of an unstable balance of forces in a

---

[1] Mestizo refers to a person of mixed Indian and white ancestry. Creole or *criollo* means an American of European ancestry.

political system dominated by mestizos in its local organization and in the army, and controlled at the top by rich creole and foreign land and mine owners. In varying degrees the same process may be observed in other countries. Out of this profound change have come the strong persistent forces which have always ultimately succeeded in overthrowing tyrannical government. This is a phenomenon in Latin American life otherwise unexplainable. In fact the very restlessness of political life, and the relentless rythym with which tyrannical dictatorships have always been overthrown are among the best evidences of the strength of the democratic urge.

On the whole, Latin American progress toward democracy during the past three or four decades has been notable. Even the wave of revolutions which began in 1930, bringing new dictators in many places, did not upset the basic trends in nations like Uruguay, Mexico, Colombia and Chile. Argentina, after a brief interlude of dictatorship, returned to the democratic fold in 1931, temporarily at least, and will return again. It now seems clear that Vargas' break with the *Integralistas* was decisive, and that Brazil will return to the democratic pattern after the war. One may well expect the next decades to be a period of substantial democratic achievement for our southern neighbor republics.

A general guide to Latin American biography is Josefina del Toro, *A Bibliography of the Collective Biography of Spanish America*, Rio Piedras, P.R., The University, 1938, 140p. (University of Puerto Rico Bulletin, series 9 no. 1). Among the collective works generally useful are Alberto Ghiraldo, *Libertadores de América*, Santiago de Chile, Ercilla, 1935; P.A. Martin, ed. *Who's Who in Latin America*, 1940 edition; W. Rex Crawford, *A Century of Latin American Thought*, Cambridge, Mass., Harvard University Press, 1944; Augusto Mijares, *Hombres e Ideas en América*, Caracas, Escuela Técnica Industrial, 1940; Álvaro Melián Lafinur, *Figuras Americanas*, Paris, Casa Editorial Franco-Ibero-Americana, 1926; William Spence Robertson, *The Rise of the Spanish-American Republics as Told in the Lives of Their Liberators*, Appleton, New York, 1918; Stewart Watt and Harold Peterson, *Builders of Latin America*, New York, Harper, 1942. Only a careful reading of the works of Latin Americans will give a real understanding of democracy in Latin America. The reader will find especially useful the works of Mijares and Crawford, mentioned above; various sections of Samuel Guy Inman's *Latin America*, revised edition, Houghton Mifflin, 1943; chapter XII in Duncan Aikman's *All American Front*, Doubleday, 1940; Víctor Andrés Belaúnde, *Bolívar and the Political Thought of the Spanish-American Revolution*, Baltimore, Johns Hopkins University Press, 1938; and A. Curtis Wilgus, ed., *South American Dictators*, Washington, George Washington University Press, 1937; Chapter XII in James Bryce, *South America*, revised edition, New York, Macmillan, 1916, is still useful.

Part I

The Movement for Independence

THE PRECURSORS AND LEADERS
OF INDEPENDENCE

An air of great unreality hangs over the early leaders of the movement for independence in Latin America. Perhaps it is because patriotic national historians have thrown over them such a veil of romanticism that they seem, somehow, to lack the flesh and blood of our Washingtons, Franklins, Adamses and Jeffersons. Yet this lack of reality seems more than simply romantic legend. It soon becomes apparent to a thoughtful student that these men have some additional characteristic, some striking trait in common, something which drove them to dream dreams impossible of realization, which they came to learn were impossible of realization, yet which led them on to attempt the impossible, and to end their lives, often, in apparent failure and disgrace.

Uniformly they failed in the task of laying stable political foundations for the new nations they had ushered into existence. Even Bolívar, San Martín and O'Higgins, who succeeded in establishing political independence, were forced to retire from political leadership in disgrace. Those like Miranda and the Carrera brothers, who failed to achieve even this first objective, frequently found their disgrace coupled with death. Those who survived were saddened, thwarted, disillusioned by the treachery and incompetence which surrounded them, and driven sometimes to the bitterest self-accusations of failure. Yet they never quite lost faith in the task they had begun. One believes, somehow, that they would have made the same attempt again, and again, if the opportunity had been given. One feels indeed, that their apparent failure was often simply an impression on their part, due to the fact that they had loosed movements and tendencies beyond their power to control. That the revolution was simply bigger than they were.

San Martín, Iturbide, perhaps Miranda, though revolutionary liberals, were monarchists at heart. So was Bernardo Vasconcellos of Brazil. Probably Hidalgo, the great Mexican revolutionist, never saw anything in liberal monarchy inconsistent with his aspirations for the liberation of the Indian and mestizo masses which followed him. Guerrero, successor to Hidalgo and Morelos as leader of the popular uprising in Mexico, could join forces with Iturbide, advocate of conservative limited monarchy, in the establishment of Mexican independence.

Obviously tradition plays an important part in such matters, especially among Hispanic peoples. In the crucial days of the uprisings of 1810 it appeared more or less clearly that the Indian and mestizo were easily swayed to support the tradition of monarchy, and that their natural sympathies leaned more in that direction than did those of the creoles. Indian and mestizo had long before learned to look to the crown for protection. It was principally the creoles who were jealous of the Spanish representatives of the crown, increasingly irritated at their exclusion from full participation in colonial government, and driven by these feelings to support Spanish American independence. Moreover, the creoles had to rely upon the Indian and mestizo, particularly the latter, for carrying through their plans for independence. It is not at all surprising, then, to find many of them, as leaders of independence, firmly convinced that a limited monarchy was the best means to achieve the political stability they desired. In the Indian and mestizo masses they recognized not only a danger to their own position and leadership, but the seeds of social and political anarchy in the days to come.

O'Higgins, Bolívar, Sucré, the Andradas, Pueyrredón, Rivadavia and others of the leaders of independence, were more thoroughly republican. They were at once more moved by the radical ideas of the French and American revolutions and less bound by traditional European concepts of government. No less cognizant than the monarchists of the practical difficulties standing in the way of democracy among their peoples, they were, nevertheless, ready to accept these difficulties and to experiment, often with radical measures, in an attempt to solve their difficulties within a republican structure of the state. To them the American Revolution and its leaders were powerful examples. This influence was in fact so great that it brought unfortunate results in many cases. Especially was this true when it led to attempts at inappropriate and impossible federalism, as in the early years of constitution making in Mexico, Colombia and elsewhere.

But at least four other factors contributed to forming Latin American constitutional ideas and practices. The French Revolution, both through its ideas of the rights of man, equality and fraternity, and through its various external manifestations in the political history of the times, was an important influence. The government of the Consulate, for example, greatly impressed Bolívar even though he turned against Napoleon after the proclamation of the Empire. The example of the British constitution was also very important. Bolívar felt the British had found the ideal way of combining traditional factors with a constitutional regime of liberty, and that the British model was suitable for a republican constitution. Just as naturally, too, both Miranda and Bolívar favored the idea of a British protectorate. The Spanish national uprising against Napoleon, and the constitutional movement which accompanied it were another strong factor. The first Chilean constitution, under O'Higgins, was based frankly upon the Spanish constitution of 1812.

A fourth factor frequently overlooked was the growing tendency, before independence, for the Spanish colonies or their ruling classes to assume direction of their own affairs in time of crisis. Examples of this political self-determinism are many, including the overthrow of a governor in Paraguay in the eighteenth century, the action of Buenos Aires in expelling the two British expeditions of 1806 and 1807, and the reactions of the leaders of Mexico and Peru to the popular uprisings in 1810 and the years following. Still another illustration may be found in the way in which the conservative leadership of Mexico reacted to the Revolution of 1820 in Spain by joining forces with the revolutionists under Guerrero.

In fact, in the final analysis, the forces of political localism usually proved stronger than the leadership of the movement for independence. Bolívar, Sucré, San Martín, Rivadavia, Iturbide all had to yield to these centrifugal and disintegrating forces, forces which appeared in the form of caudillos or strong men with power derived from the militarism of the long chaotic years (1810-1825) of the wars for independence. During these years, it is well to remember, an entire generation grew up knowing no other authority than that of local military leaders. As a result, the first generation of political leadership in Latin America was crushed between the forces of localism, predominantly mestizo, and the reactionary elements in the church and landowning gentry, surrendering, usually, to the former.

In the midst of this political chaos and disintegration an autonomous pattern of political organization began to appear, particularly in Spanish America. This autonomous tendency, which pointed in some respects toward liberal monarchy, had already been strong enough in the late eighteenth century to bring forth Aranda's famous proposal for erecting the viceroyalties into autonomous kingdoms under separate princes of the Bourbon line, a proposal seconded by Prince Godoy twenty years later. This unconscious tendency toward autonomy within the Spanish pattern of government must have exercised great influence on the schemes of Miranda and Bolívar and is especially noticeable in San Martín. It has been important, also since Independence, in the development of republican institutions. In fact this autonomous, American characteristic is fundamental to the basic type of Spanish American political institution today, a type of state visualized clearly by Alberdi: centralized, with a powerful executive, and with the characteristically Spanish refusal to admit a clearcut separation of powers. How strongly indigenous this autonomous type is, was shown often during the past century in its constant reassertion against any imported pattern of government which happened to have been written into formal constitutions.

Although long delayed in Brazil, republican leadership triumphed eventually throughout Latin America. But the first attempts at political organization were mostly tragic failures. The generation of 1810 failed to give even stable political structures to their fledgling nations. The failure was due in part to outside influences from Britain, the United States, and Europe, and in part to factors of political localism. Yet in spite of these initial failures republican leadership continued vigorously.

Except for the balance of power in Europe and the blessing of Great Britain, the Latin American experiments in republican self-government might have been impossible. Yet they are not simply the result of the Old World balance of power. One must also see in them the same New World desire, often unconscious and unexpressed, which animated the North American colonists in their struggle to secure a government of their own creation and under their own control which would secure for them and their posterity the blessings of freedom, and insure the rights of life, liberty and the pursuit of happiness. This fact stands out above everything else in the biographical sketches which follow.

Francisco de Miranda (1752?-1816)

The Precursor

Francisco de Miranda, more than any other Latin American of his day personifies the history of Latin America during the three decades between the American Revolution and the Declaration of Venezuelan Independence in 1811. A Venezuelan creole, scion of a prominent Caracas family, officer in the Spanish army, his service against the English during the American Revolution was the beginning of a life-long revolutionary career. Immersed in the large and liberal ideas of his day, he saw in the French Revolution the coming of a new age, and eagerly entered the Revolutionary army. Like some other military leaders of the time he narrowly escaped death at the hands of the revolutionary tribunals. Friend and admirer of the leaders of the American Revolution, he was an equally great admirer of the British constitution. Although he played casually with most of the plans for social regeneration current in his day, his greatest dream was that of creating new states in Spanish America on the British model, and under the protection of the British crown.

Although of only average height, Miranda was a large man. Contemporaries agree that he made a handsome and imposing figure and gave the impression of great physical vigor. His hazel eyes were at once penetrating and commanding and contributed to the haughty, almost forbidding look in his portrait. He looked much like a Spanish grandee loyally serving the cause of Ferdinand VII. Yet no other Latin American during his lifetime was more closely associated with the liberal and revolutionary forces of his day. Indeed, his career touched the three great phases of the American-French Revolutionary period: the American Revolution, the French Revolution and the Wars of Latin American Independence.

It was the Argentine soldier, president and historian, Bartolomé Mitre, who in his *History of Belgrano*, pointed to Miranda as the precursor of Latin American independence. Later historians have followed Mitre's lead. The Venezuelan Congress bestowed the title upon him posthumously, and few today would question his right to the distinction.

The exact date of his birth is not known with certainty, but Francisco de Miranda was born about 1752, in Caracas, the birthplace of Bolívar and Andrés Bello. He was the son of Sebastian de Miranda, well-to-do merchant and militia officer, and Francisca Antonia Rodríguez de Espiñosa. Because of his family position, he received a good education in the College and Royal University of Santa Rosa in Caracas, and probably spent a year study-

ing in the City of Mexico.   At an early age he went to Spain, where, presumably after study in a military school, he received a commission in the
Spanish army, probably by purchase.   After brief service in North Africa,
he was assigned, in 1780, to the expedition sent to America to participate
in the war against the English.   After the war, he with his superior, Cacigal,
was accused of treason against the Spanish crown, because of certain mys-
terious transactions in Jamaica.   He managed to escape from Havana to
the United States, however, and began his friendship with such prominent
North Americans as Adams, Jefferson, Knox, and later, Washington.

Miranda speaks of the next period in his life as one of "traveling to
correct the deficiencies of his education."   It would be more accurate to speak
of it as a period of preparation for the work of liberating Spanish America.
With his trial for treason still pending before the Spanish court he traveled
to England.   At once he began to suggest to leaders in British life the
possibilities of Spanish American independence.   Accompanied by the American Colonel William S. Smith, he visited Holland, Denmark, Norway,
Sweden, Germany, Russia, Switzerland, France, Italy, and   Turkey, going
as far into the Middle East as Asia Minor.   He visited Frederick the Great,
Mendelssohn, Haydn, and Catherine the Great, and cultivated the acquaintance of Potemkin.   Miranda's projects were gradually assuming broader scope
and one object of his travels was to secure assurance in European courts of
support for his American plans.   He succeeded at least in winning the
personal support of the great Russian empress.

Back in England, the Nootka Sound controversy between Spain and
England provided the opportunity for his first proposal for Latin American
independence.   William Pitt was apparently interested, but finally offered no
aid.   Just about this time the French Revolution swept Miranda into its orbit.
As a general of the French Republic, he led an army into Belgium, and
became its military governor.   The treason of Dumouriez, however, brought
his recall to Paris, and a long imprisonment.   Yet in spite of the apparent
hostility of Danton, Marat, and Robespierre he was acquitted.   During the
years which followed, he was constantly involved in a series of plans and
intrigues with French revolutionary leaders in which he figured as the poten-
tial leader of independence in America under French protection.   Imprisoned
again by Robespierre, he was released in the Thermidorian reaction.   Arrested
again by the Directory, he was released and ordered to leave the country, but
still stayed on in France until 1798 when he returned to England.

Thereafter his time was divided between planning American independence through the revolutionary lodges, and teaching.   Among his students
was young Bernardo O'Higgins, son of the Viceroy of Peru, who came to
him in search of a teacher of mathematics.   Miranda introduced young
O'Higgins to the society of the revolutionary lodges, and thus began the

young Chilean's revolutionary career. However much mathematics he may have implanted in the mind of his young disciple, he certainly filled him with the determination to achieve the liberation of Spanish America. Twenty years later his teaching bore fruit in the independence of Chile.

When in 1798 Miranda reappeared opportunely in England, the hostility of Britain to France and Spain and the undeclared naval war of the United States against France played into his hands. It is the considered opinion of William Spence Robertson that except for the stubbornness of Adams and Pickering, England and the United States might have joined hands in 1798 or 1799 in support of Miranda's plan for the liberation of Spanish America.

The death of William Pitt thwarted his plans again in 1805 just when they seemed on the point of going through, and led to his ill-fated attempt in 1806 to land on the Venezuelan coast, an attempt doomed to failure from the outset because of the lack of proper preparation and support. But his greatest disappointment came in 1808 when the expedition prepared under Wellesley to liberate Spanish America, was sent into Portugal and Spain, instead.

Yet, even after twenty years of failure, Miranda did not give up hope. At last his opportunity seemed to come when the revolution of 1810 brought uprising throughout the Spanish colonies in the name of the deposed Ferdinand VII. Young Simón Bolívar, visiting in England, encouraged him to return to his native Venezuela.

Here his influence in the Venezuelan Congress, more than that of any other individual, brought the Declaration of Independence in 1811. His influence was also decisive in shaping the new constitution, even though the plan finally agreed upon included many factors with which he disagreed, especially the federalism copied from the United States.

Miranda was justifiably skeptical of the practicability of federalism, and urged instead a central republic. Suffrage, he felt, should be restricted to those who could read and write, owned property and had never been employed in domestic service. Yet he believed in emancipation of the slaves, and cultivated the favor of the Negroes liberated under the first Venezuelan republic. From 1790 on he had urged federation of all the provinces of Spanish America, once liberated. This idea from the United States Constitution was reflected in the Venezuelan Constitution in its provision for admission of other American States into the union.

The disastrous earthquake of 1812 brought a superstitious revulsion of Venezuelan feeling against the revolutionary government. This feeling was capitalized, naturally, by reactionary leaders who were dismayed at the radical turn the new government was taking. In accordance with the provision of the constitution, the friends of independence made Miranda a temporary dictator to stem this rising rebellion. But the task was hopeless.

Capture by the royalists of the fort at Puerto Cabello, commanded by young Bolívar, proved disastrous to the movement for independence. Miranda decided to surrender to prevent further bloodshed. Then followed one of the most tragic incidents in the history of Latin America. On the eve of the day Miranda and his party planned to embark from La Guayra upon a British vessel of war, he was turned over to the loyalist general Monteverde by Bolívar, the commander of the port, whom he had supposed to be loyal. It is one of the enigmas in the life of Bolívar. He apparently felt that Miranda had traitorously betrayed the revolutionary cause, but his motives are by no means entirely clear. Miranda lived on in a Spanish prison until July 14, 1816, never giving up hope of escape, nor hope of success in freeing Latin America.

He was typical of his times—doctrinaire, inconsistent, opportunistic, at times unscrupulous. As a soldier his military experience was wide and various. Yet it is as a military leader that he has been most frequently criticized even by his followers. His real genius was for the instigation of revolution, and for complicated intrigues of the kind he was constantly instigating while in France and England. Yet his chief historical importance must be sought outside the realm of military, and even of political, leadership in the usual sense. Miranda's real secret was that he made himself the embodiment, the personification of the idea of Latin American independence during a quarter of a century. In Latin America Miranda *was* the Revolution, and it is in this sense that he is the great "Precursor."

Crane, John and Wilgus, A. C. General Francisco Miranda; the forerunner of South American Independence. Washington, American Patriots Series. 1942. 16p.

Ghiraldo, Alberto. Libertadores de América. Santiago de Chile, Ercilla. 1935. p63-6.

Nucete-Sardi, José. Aventura y tragedia de Don Francisco de Miranda. Caracas, Cooperativa de Artes Gráficas. 1935. 415p.

Parra Pérez, Caracciolo. Historia de la primera república de Venezuela. Caracas, Tipografía Americana. 1939. 2v.

Parra Pérez, Caracciolo. Miranda et la revolution francaise. Paris, J. Desmoulins. 1925. 474p.

Robertson, William Spence, ed. The diary of Francisco de Miranda, tour of the United States, 1783-1784. New York, Hispanic Society of America. 1928. 206p. Spanish text edited with introduction and notes by William Spence Robertson.

Robertson, William Spence, ed. The life of Miranda. Chapel Hill, University of North Carolina Press. 1930. 2v.

Watt, Stewart and Peterson, H. F. Builders of Latin America. New York and London, Harper & Brothers. 1942. p92-105

Simón Bolívar (1783-1830)

The Liberator

No other character in the history of Latin America is so well known and at the same time so little understood as Simón Bolívar. He was the liberator of five republics, a great soldier, statesman, constitution maker and law giver, yet he is most often represented in history as a megalomaniac. By some historians he is described as a man who, in his boldest moments, and at the apogee of his power, dreamed of an imperial crown and of wielding a scepter energetically. By others he is represented in the tragic, romantic role of one who sees his highest and fondest dreams and plans shattered, his work destroyed by the faithlessness and smallness of the little military chieftains. He is represented as a soul in anguish over the conflict of his ideals with the political course to which he was forced by the caudillos, whose political vision was limited to the concept of personal rule by strong-arm methods in their own little communities. He is shown to us, betrayed by his comrades, accused of ambition to wield a scepter, broken hearted because of the failure of his plan for union of the countries of northern South America, deposed and exiled, tragically disillusioned at last, lamenting on his death bed: "I have ploughed the sea."

Yet none of these is the true Bolívar, nor the whole Bolívar. None of these is the Bolívar who saw the realities and the limitations of Latin American political life while he fought for its independence, who continued to believe in its future possibilities, continued to believe in democracy, and to forge institutions and laws for its development.

The great Liberator was born in Caracas, Venezuela, on July 24, 1783, one year and nine months after the British surrender at Yorktown. His father was a wealthy marquis of Basque origin, owner of rich copper and silver mines in the mountains and of great plantations in the fertile valleys. Some Negro historians have tried to prove that he was part Negro, but the point has never been well substantiated. Simón inherited over a thousand slaves, and on the day of his baptism received an estate which yielded an annual income of twenty thousand pesos. His father died when Simón was three, and his early education was entrusted to the unkempt, eccentric philosopher, Simón Rodríguez, who missed no opportunity to instill in the mind of his young charge ideas derived from his beloved eighteenth century French philosophers, and hatred of all things Spanish. Going to Spain to study at the age of sixteen, Bolívar lived the characteristic life of a wealthy young student. Yet gradually he became more and more imbued with the idea of liberating his native Venezuela. To his youthful eyes the France of Napoleon's Consulate seemed at this time the ideal solution for his fatherland. Yet when he returned to Europe a few years later, after the tragic death of his young bride, the beautiful Maria Teresa, to find Napoleon assuming a crown, he condemned his former idol as a "tyrant, a hypocrite, and an obstacle to liberty and progress," and refused an invitation to the coronation ceremonies.

In this European environment he lived a life of fashion, acquiring a great reputation for fastidiousness. A hat was named for him. Then, one day in Rome, he went with his tutor to visit the Aventine Hill. There, very dramatically, he swore never to rest until he had broken the chains of Spanish rule. True to his romantic vow, a few years later he was one of the little group led by Francisco de Miranda, which established the first Venezuelan Republic. He was twenty-eight when he made a fiery speech which brought the proclamation of Venezuelan independence in 1811, and only twenty-nine when the collapse of the republic after the ill-fated earthquake of 1812 threw the leadership of the whole Venezuelan movement, and shortly afterward the Colombia movement as well, into his hands.

The next seven years were years of bitter frustration and defeat, years which tested the soul of the great Liberator as few leaders in history have been tested. Yet in 1815, in the midst of defeat, his estates confiscated, deserted and reviled by his friends and comrades, he could still pen from Jamaica a letter which is one of the classics of American political thought, breathing unquestioning confidence in the ultimate triumph of the republican movement, in spite of the many obstacles which he saw lying in the path of democracy.

In 1819 he initiated the successful military campaign which brought independence to Venezuela and Colombia, and their union within the next two years. By 1826, standing at the height of his success and power, he had established the independence of Venezuela, Colombia, Peru, and Bolivia. Then followed four years of the most disastrous failure and the collapse of all his great projects. They were years of anguish which saw the breakup of the projected union of Greater Colombia, desertion and betrayal by his friends, and an attempt upon his life which failed only because of the loyalty and bravery of his mistress. Then came political ostracism and exile, and finally his death in 1830, a broken and ruined man.

Bolívar undoubtedly died believing himself a failure. But did he retain belief in the ideals for which he fought? "Jesus Christ, Don Quixote and I have been the three greatest fools of history," he is supposed to have said in his bitterness. But the judgment of history must be different. For Bolívar was realist enough to see that neither the federalism of the United States, nor the monarchism of San Martín could solve the problem of organizing free governments among his people. He was greatly influenced by the British constitutional monarchy and desired a British protectorate. In the Plan of

Angostura, and in the Bolivian constitution of which he was the author, he provided a life term presidency, a kind of "monarchy in disguise," a hereditary senate composed of the revolutionary leaders, "the elite of state and war," and a fourth, or *Moral* power, to be exercised by censors holding office for life. The responsibility of the moral power was to prepare the population for citizenship in a democracy. It was a kind of glorified combination of a department of education and a modern department of propaganda.

He staked his whole success on a projected union of countries based on these principles, and died feeling his whole work had been undone by shorter-sighted leaders. Yet out of the bitterness of the next century of struggle for stable government in Latin America came a slow realization that he had seen clearly where others fumbled for the solution. And still, today, one who has not looked at Latin American democracy through the eyes of Bolívar cannot make sense out of its apparent anomalies. Anyone reading his Jamaica letter today for the first time could almost feel he had a gift of clairvoyance, so accurately did he forecast the social and political problems of the new Latin American states then struggling into existence, so clearly did he see the geographic significance of the Isthmus of Panama and its importance for the entire continent.

Alvarez del Vayo, Julio. Simón Bolívar. *In* Ludwig, Emil and Kranz, H. B. The torch of freedom. New York, Farrar and Rinehart. 1943. p107-28.

Angell, Hildegarde. Simón Bolívar, South American liberator. New York, Norton. 1930. 296p.

Baker, Nina B. He wouldn't be king. New York, Vanguard. 1941. 305p.

Belaúnde, Víctor Andrés. Bolívar and the political thought of the Spanish-American revolution. Baltimore, Johns Hopkins Press. 1938. 451p.

Bibliography of the liberator Simón Bolívar. Washington, Pan American Union. 1930. 22p. (Bibliography Series, No. 1. Mimeographed).

Bolívar, Simón. . . . Doctrina política: Carta de Jamaica, Discurso de Angostura, Preámbulo a la constitución boliviana. Prólogo y notas de Luis Alberto Sánchez. Santiago de Chile, Ercilla. 1940. 129p.

Crane, John and Wilgus, A. C. General Simón Bolívar, the great South American liberator. Washington, American Patriots Series. 1942. 15p.

Ghiraldo, Alberto. Libertadores de América. Santiago de Chile, Ercilla. 1935. p. 31-9.

Larrazábal, Felipe. La vida y correspondencia general del libertador Simón Bolívar. New York, Andres Cassard. 1883. 2v.

Ludwig, Emil. Bolívar, the life of an idealist. New York, Alliance Book Co. 1942. 362p.

Mancini, Jules. Bolívar y la emancipación de las colonias españolas. Selection in English translation *in* Arciniegas, Germán, ed. The green continent. New York, Knopf. 1944. p247-63. Original text in French.

Robertson, William Spence. Rise of the Spanish-American republics. New York, Appleton. 1919. 380p.

Waugh, Elizabeth D. Simon Bolivar. New York. Macmillan. 1941. 326p.

José de San Martín (1778-1850)

The Soldier Statesman

If San Martín had had his way the twenty Latin American republics would today be a much smaller number of limited, liberal monarchies, presided over by constitutional sovereigns selected from the house of Brunswick, or Braganza, or even from some branch of the Spanish Bourbon family. Liberator of all of southern South America and a greater military leader than Simón Bolívar, San Martín also had more of the spirit of abnegation than his great northern rival. In fact he had no political ambitions. Yet, like Bolívar he could not think of strong stable government being achieved under the petty, selfish military chiefs who were springing up in every locality in the wake of the War of Independence. Like Bolívar he staked all on a plan, the plan of introducing European princes with the understanding and support of European powers. Like Bolívar, he saw his plan fail, opposed even by his most faithful lieutenant, O'Higgins, and withdrew into exile and oblivion, his great services all but forgotten by the republics he had created.

José de San Martín was born February 25, 1778, in the little village of Yapeyu, in the present state of Corrientes, Argentina. His father was a Spanish official, his mother a creole from one of the finest families of Buenos Aires. He studied in the little mission school for the Indians and mestizos of the village, and in Buenos Aires, until the age of eight, when he was taken by his parents to Spain. There he was enrolled in the Seminary for Nobles of Madrid. His real education began when at the age of eleven, he became a cadet in the Murcian regiment, and for the next thirty-four years his life was that of a soldier. By the time he was seventeen he was a second lieutenant under the gallant General Ricardo, from whose campaigns against the French he learned early the brilliant tactics he was later to use so successfully in America.

He fought through the wars of the French Revolution, against France, and against Britain; was captured by the English in the naval engagement off Cape San Vicente in 1798; headed a company of his Murcian regiment in the war against Portugal in 1801; took part in the siege of Gibraltar and Ceuta, and in the occupation of Portugal under the Treaty of Fontainbleau. But it was after 1808, in the war of the Spanish patriots against Joseph Bonaparte and the French, that he became known throughout Europe as a brilliant leader of guerrillas.

Twenty-two years of constant warfare, in contact with the best generals of Europe, had made him, at the age of thirty-three, one of the most skilled and experienced military tacticians of his day. His sympathy for his native Argentina was still strong, and this sympathy was to be the springboard for the still greater success which lay ahead. For somehow, moved by the experiences of the Spanish war of liberation, he had decided to throw in his lot with the cause of Argentine liberation.

Lord MacDuff, who had fought for the Spanish cause, secured him a passport for England. There he soon met the group of Latin Americans which Miranda had formed into a secret society, all pledged to the cause of liberty. With their help and enthusiastic encouragement he planned his departure for Buenos Aires in January 1812.

The Argentine revolution had begun two years before with the famous "Cry" of May 25, 1810, but it still lacked solid political and military organization, and above all, military leadership. For this reason, especially, San Martín was welcomed by the triumvirate of 1812 headed by Rivadavia, confirmed in his rank of lieutenant colonel, and immediately assigned the task of organizing a squadron of cavalry. He carried out this first assignment so well, infusing into the men his own cold fanatical courage, that he was immediately authorized to form a regiment of cavalry. This was the regiment which history knows as the famous Grenadiers of San Martín, the regiment which followed him faithfully and with unfailing success, through all his American campaigns.

After his first success in the Battle of Lorenzo, San Martín was given charge of the main army of the north, whose job it was to drive the Spaniards from Upper Peru. Under Belgrano the northern army had won some initial successes, only to meet later with thoroughly demoralizing defeat. San Martín formed the daring plan of out-flanking the main Spanish forces in Upper Peru by the liberation of Chile, then attacking Peru by sea, while at the same time supporting agitation for a revolt in Upper Peru. His strategy was overwhelmingly successful. Chile was liberated by 1819 through the brilliant victories of Chacabuco and Maipú. By 1820, with the aid of Lord Cochrane, San Martín was ready to invade Peru by sea. This move, too, was completed with success, Lima was occupied, and the independence of Peru proclaimed.

But at this point San Martín seemed content to stop. Perhaps he was unable to pursue his initial advantage by attacking the Spaniards back in the mountains. More than likely he did not wish to. He now wished to negotiate for the establishment of a European prince or princes in America. By this means, with British support he hoped to secure Spanish recognition of Latin American independence. As late as 1822 he dispatched two deputies to Chile and Argentina asking support for such a plan. The political situation in Europe was rapidly changing, however, as the Council of Verona was soon to indicate, and there was no liklihood of finding substantial support for his design in Europe. American support was still less likely.

Just at this juncture the armies of Bolívar appeared on the northern horizon, flushed with the liberation of Colombia, Venezuela and Ecuador.

The meeting of San Martín and Bolívar which followed at Guayaquil provides us with one of the most dramatic moments in American history. Perhaps historians have romanticized too much San Martín's spirit of abnegation in this conference. Certainly he renounced the dream of political power which the less self-effacing Bolívar pursued to his own misery. Yet one should not overlook another significance of this famous conference. To San Martín it was the end of the possibility of limited monarchy in America, and so the end of his effective participation as a political leader in the formation of the newly born nations.

San Martín was a great soldier. Of the trilogy of great military leaders of American independence, Washington, Bolívar, and San Martín, he is perhaps the greatest. Moreover, he was a political realist who foresaw the dismal depths of caudillism and personalism to which Latin American political life could and did descend.

He felt strongly that the Latin American states could only achieve stability through European monarchy. In later years he admitted that Chile proved an exception to the rule. But he was wrong in respect to the rest of Latin America as well. Gropingly the Latin American would find a better, because a more American solution. European princes, undoubtedly, would have met in every Spanish American country the same unhappy fate that Maximilian met in Mexico. San Martín's greatest contribution to Latin American democracy, clearly, was not his formula for political organization. Aside from the military leadership he provided, his greatest contribution was the example of supreme self-abnegation he set by voluntarily withdrawing from political power. Perhaps, more than anything else he did, this example helped to make possible the very kind of self-government in Latin America which he had believed impossible.

Crane, John and Wilgus, A. C. General San Martín, the savior of the south. Washington, American Patriots Series. 1942. 16p.

Ghiraldo, Alberto. Libertadores de América. Santiago de Chile, Ercilla. 1935. p7-29.

Harrison, Margaret H. Captain of the Andes, the life of Don José de San Martín, liberator of Argentine, Chile and Peru. New York, Richard H. Smith. 1943. 216p.

Robertson, William Spence. Rise of the Spanish-American republics. New York, Appleton. 1919. 380p.

Rojas, Ricardo. El santo de la espada, Buenos Aires, 1933. Selection in English translation in Arciniegas, Germán, ed. The green continent. New York, Knopf. 1944. p268-85.

La Prensa. Dec. 12, 1942. Los últimos días del libertador en Chile. Juan Estevan Guastavino.

BERNARDO O'HIGGINS (1778?-1842)

Founder of Chile

Chile was the first of the Spanish American nations to achieve stable constitutional government, as well as the first to develop a merchant marine and a navy. With both these distinctive accomplishments the name of Bernardo O'Higgins is closely linked. This undeviating devotee of the principles of republicanism unquestionably belongs in any galaxy of great American statesmen.

Unlike his great collaborator, San Martín, O'Higgins was unswerving in opposition to monarchy, and unlike Bolívar he refused to resort to dictatorship to force his constitution on an unwilling country. His voluntary resignation in 1823, when he might easily have suppressed the opposition with his loyal troops, is hailed by Chilean historians as a great act of abnegation which did much to insure political stability and democracy in Chile.

Bernardo O'Higgins was born August 20, 1778 [1] in Chillan, Chile, the illegitimate son of the fifteen-year-old daughter of a prominant Chilean family and a remarkable Irish immigrant father then sixty years of age. His mother, Isabel Requelme, later married a neighbor, Felix Rodríguez. Ambrose O'Higgins, the father, had been sent to Buenos Aires from Ireland at an early age by his uncle, a priest. It may be a legend that he first made his way as a peddler in the Argentine. Whatever his beginning, he rose rapidly in the Chilean army, with the support of the great minister, José de Gálvez, and finally became Captain General of Chile. Later he received the title of Marquis of Osorno, held the office of viceroy, and attained great wealth. Ambrose O'Higgins' Negro mistress (not the mother of Bernardo) was one of the scandals of the day in conservative Santiago society.

When Bernardo was fourteen he was sent to Lima to study. Four years later he was sent to Spain and England, in the days of the Consulate. The normal effect upon an impressionable youth of eighteen is readily imaginable. Naturally he responded to the enthusiasm, the idealism, the optimism which still animated the revolutionary leaders, even though the first enthusiasm of the Republic was gone. A further unsettling factor in Bernardo's case, was a disagreement over financial matters with his father's agent in Cadiz. This disagreement brought him back to Spain and eventually to America. Meanwhile he spent several happy years of study in England. Toward the end of his stay there he engaged Francisco de Miranda as tutor in mathematics, thus

---

[1] There is some uncertainty about this date. Mackenna says 1780.

beginning a strong friendship which also brought him into association with a group of Latin Americans in England devoted to the cause of freedom and Spanish American independence. Bernardo soon became imbued with their ideas and enthusiasm, and when he returned to Spain, it was partly in the role of a revolutionary emissary.

O'Higgins returned to Chile in 1802, having committed to memory Miranda's secret "decalog" of revolutionary precepts. In 1803 the death of his father left him a man of great wealth and he devoted himself thereafter to its management. Meanwhile, in accordance with Miranda's advice, he cultivated the friendship of men of liberal views in Chile. When the revolt against the Spanish authorities began in 1810, the son of a former viceroy was an important acquisition to the patriot cause, and O'Higgins, as Alcalde of Chillan, quickly became one of its chief leaders. Moreover, he immediately demonstrated his ability as a daring and determined military leader. In 1813 he became commander-in-chief of the patriot army.

In spite of early success, the patriots were defeated in the fatal battle of Rancagua in 1814 by an army sent from Peru. O'Higgins and his followers took refuge across the Andes in Mendoza, Argentina. There they joined forces with General San Martín in organizing the army which returned to Chile two years later, defeated the Spaniards in the battles of Chacabuco and Maipú and established Chilean independence. O'Higgins was immediately proclaimed Director of Chile, and busied himself with the double task of organizing the new nation and cooperating with San Martín in the preparation of the army and fleet to be sent against Peru.

Without question, O'Higgins is the greatest military figure in the movement for Chilean independence, and second only to the great professional soldier, San Martín, in the whole movement for the liberation of southern South America. There is less agreement about O'Higgins in civil life in the role of statesman and ruler. He wanted to see his whole liberal program applied at once, and impatiently pushed his plans for social, educational, commercial and religious reform more rapidly than his more conservative supporters wished to go. Refusing firmly the monarchism of San Martín, even when the Chilean Congress favored it, he adopted, instead, the liberal constitutional ideas of his friend, Rodríguez Aldea. The resulting Constitution of 1822 was derived basically from the liberal Spanish constitution of 1812, and contained many advanced liberal provisions. As in the Bolivarian constitutions, the office of director was a powerful one, with most of the attributes of kingship, even to the inviolability of person, and the required consent of congress for the director's marriage.

O'Higgins' rule under the new Constitution came to grief partly because of the conservative opposition aroused by his educational and church reforms. Another cause was the extreme unpopularity of Rodríguez Aldea, who as minister of hacienda exercised great influence in the government. In addition charges of abuse of power came to be made against O'Higgins himself, some of them unfounded, some of them the unauthorized acts of his subordinates. He was also accused, unjustly in this case, of the death of the great revolutionary leaders, the Carrera brothers. The suspicion was a natural one since it was known he had never forgiven them for the defeat at Rancagua, nor for the death in a duel of his personal friend, Juan Mackenna.

Although these charges were largely unfounded, it reflects seriously on O'Higgins' capacity as a ruler that he allowed such unfounded rumours to create an impossible political situation. The result was his resignation in such apparent failure that it has provided Chilean historians with one of their classical controversies. Yet O'Higgins gave one last clear demonstration of his devotion to democratic principles. Faced with revolt in 1823, and with a hostile meeting of citizens in Santiago calling for his resignation, he accepted failure, yielded to the public will, and resigned rather than use the military force which he controlled and with which he could have suppressed the opposition.

Ostracised, a lonely exile, he spent the next twenty years living in poverty in Peru, until his death in 1842. He refrained from participation in counter-revolutionary schemes, in spite of the frequent demands of malcontents. There was no bitterness in his soul and he rejoiced in Chile's rapid achievement of political stability under the leadership of his conservative opponents. It is this voluntary withdrawal, this act of abnegation so similar to that of San Martín, which causes the historians of his country to call him the greatest civic figure in the movement for independence in Chile. Perhaps it was his greatest contribution to the making of Chilean democracy.

Donoso, Ricardo. General Bernardo O'Higgins. Washington, Pan American Union. n.d. 8p. (Tr. by Frances Douglas)

Ghiraldo, Alberto. Libertadores de América. Santiago de Chile, Ercilla. 1935. p45-8.

Vicuña Mackenna, Benjamín. Vida de O'Higgins, in Obras completas de Vicuña Mackenna, v5. Santiago de Chile, University of Chile. 1936.

BERNARDO DE MONTEAGUDO (1785-1825)

Propagandist for Democracy and Pan Americanism

Bernardo Monteagudo, follower and protegé of San Martín, represents in his own life many of the complicated forces and tendencies behind the Spanish American movement for independence. Although not a military leader, he was a man of action, who did more than some of the military leaders to win South American independence.

Historians have disagreed over his personal character. Some represent him as malignant, perverted, Borgia-like, others as the incorporation of the spirit of liberal reform. Yet no one refuses to recognize his merit and his substantial contribution to the propaganda which made the revolution in America a success, and to the creation of democratic institutions in the newly independent American nations. One Argentine has called him a Jacobin transplanted to America to give impulse with his democratic enthusiasm to the cause of independence. Another (Alberto Ghiraldo) has called him the "demagog of the Revolution." All, moreover, recognize him as the first great propagandist for Pan Americanism.

Like others of the early Latin American leaders, his romantic spirit of democratic revolt and over-optimistic liberalism led him to attempt rash measures. Like them, too, he was frequently inconsistent, opportunistic. Yet certainly no one saw more clearly than Monteagudo that effective independence in Latin America would require and bring basic social change. This was the secret of his success in winning support for the democratic cause: his perception of the social changes implicit in independence.

Although the place and date of his birth have not been accepted without argument, it is probable that he was born in Tucumán, Argentina, in 1785. An Argentine biographer has asserted that he was a mulatto, but this is far from certain. Considering the region of his birth, it is unlikely. Ricardo Rojas has written in his edition of Monteagudo's works that he had "black and fiery eyes in the swarthy and pallid countenance of a man of Tucumán." His parents were Miguel Monteagudo and Catalina Cáceres. Little is known concerning Miguel Monteagudo, except his will. He seems, however, to have possessed enough means to give a good education to his son Bernardo, the only child of ten to survive infancy. Bernardo studied in the University of Córdoba and later in that of Chuquisaca, where he received a doctoral degree in 1808. Here the movement for independence found him.

The first phase of his active participation in political life began with the uprising in Chuquisaca in 1809. Condemned to death for participation in the uprising, he fled to Buenos Aires, joined the patriot army and took an active part in the early phases of the war. What first made him the object of great attention, however, was his defense of the patriot leader Castelli against the charges made after the military campaign which ended in the disastrous defeat of the *Desaguadero*. His bold defense, published in Buenos Aires in the *Gaceta* already made famous by Mariano Moreno, marked the beginning of Monteagudo's active collaboration in that journal. During the next few years, following the precedent set by Moreno, he made it the organ of the revolutionary movement. After suppression of the *Gaceta* he founded a new journal, *Mártir o Libre* (Martyr or Freeman) to continue his liberal agitation.

While many faltered and were uncertain on the question of independence, Monteagudo in the *Gaceta*, in his speeches before the Sociedad Patriótica, which he assisted in founding, and in his short-lived journal, *Mártir o Libre*, never hesitated. From the beginning, and insistently, until the Congress of Tucumán in 1816, he urged an immediate declaration of independence, a declaration "that we are in the just possession of our rights."

His creed was simple. Spanish influence and institutions had to be stamped out if tyranny was to be ended and enslaved men set free. There would be no tyrants if there were no slaves. The break should be complete, for only a republic could unite freedom loving individuals in opposition to tyranny. But more than this was necessary, too. While public opinion was the most powerful force in the world, he saw also the necessity of certain leaders, "so determined to die for the cause of humanity that they never fear the fury of tyrants, the caprice of factions, nor even the influence of their own friends." The violence of his language against tyrants approached the intense fury of Marat.

He urged freedom of speech and freedom of the press. The press, he thought, could exercise a censor's function over the government. Every man over twenty who could read and write, exercised some profession, was not subject to the control of another and had not been convicted of crime, should exercise the rights of citizenship. Ignorance he saw as the principal source of man's misfortunes and so, while in Lima, he urged the necessity for general education. He advocated freedom of commerce, and was confident that America stood at the dawn of her day, while Europe stood at the setting of the sun. In 1812 he wrote, "Numerous cities will emerge from the bosom of these immense deserts; our ships will cover the seas, abundance will reign within our walls and two words only will be seen over our altars and in our tribunals: *humanity and liberty*."

Federalism as the constitutional basis for Latin America he considered a dangerous experiment under conditions then existing, even though it might become possible in the future. He was insistent that sovereignty resided

in the people, and authority in laws. Yet he saw the necessity of a strong
single executive if legislative abuses were to be avoided and a stable constitution achieved.

He was an official in Argentina at the time of the conspiracy of Alzoga,
and represented the province of Mendoza in the assembly of 1813. Again
he was editing the *Gaceta*, making of it an urgent voice of reform. By this
time, too, he had attached himself to the fortunes of Alvear, the Supreme
Director of Argentina. The fall of the latter, which quickly ensued, brought
Monteagudo's temporary eclipse, and his exile from Argentina.

After traveling through Brazil and Europe, he reappeared in Chile with
San Martín's expedition. San Martín recognized his genius and gave him
his fullest confidence. As San Martín's secretary, he prepared official papers
and proclamations, and had general charge of propaganda. It was thus
that he wrote the Chilean Declaration of Independence in 1818. In the
controversy which ensued between the Carrera brothers and Bernardo O'Higgins, Monteagudo identified himself with O'Higgins.

Yet he followed San Martín to Peru and became his most energetic
and able minister in the government of the Protectorate there. He under-
took basic reforms of the legal system, abolished slavery, and separated
Church and State: measures which quickly aroused violent opposition in conservative Peru, especially among Spanish elements. The defense of his
actions in Peru is to be found in his *Memoria*, one of the important docu-
ments in the history of American democracy. The forces of reaction were
too strong, however, and at the first opportunity presented by San Martín's
absence he was exiled and sent on a warship to Panama. Then, surprisingly,
he managed to join Bolívar in Quito. In spite of the decree of exile he
then returned to Peru with the Liberator.

The triumph of his return was short lived. He barely had time to write
the "Essay on the Necessity of a General Federation Among the Hispanic
American States," before he fell the victim of an assassin's dagger in Lima
in 1825. The essay on Hispanic American union was intended to be the
basis for Bolívar's proposed Congress of the American States at Panama.
Monteagudo had long urged the desirability of a union of the Spanish
American states in their opposition to Spain, and his arguments undoubtedly
had helped to convince Bolívar of the desirability of such a union. Authorship of this essay, alone, would be enough claim to fame even if Monteagudo
had not wielded one of the most forceful liberal pens of the period of
independence. All things considered, it is doubtful whether either the great
Bolívar or the journalist Moreno was a more effective propagandist for
democracy, independence and Pan Americanism than this brilliant and ill-
fated Argentine leader of the early movement for democracy in Argentina,
Chile and Peru.

Ghiraldo, Alberto. Libertadores de América. Santiago de Chile, Ercilla. 1935. p89-92.

Melián Lafinur, Álvaro. Figuras Americanas. Paris, Casa Editorial Franco-Ibero-Americana. 1926. p31-47.

Moses, Bernard. The intellectual background of the revolution in South America, 1810-1824. New York, Hispanic Society of America. 1926. p86-95, 109-16.

José Bonifacio de Andrada e Silva (1763-1838)

Patriarch of Brazilian Independence

The empire of Brazil under Pedro I, and during the regency for Pedro II, has often been called the Empire of José Bonifacio. And aptly, for the great mineralogist, naturalist and former professor of the University of Coimbra, who refused royal decorations, and asked to have inscribed on his tomb that his only honor was that of loving his land and his people, was the statesman, more than any other, who fashioned the independence of Brazil. Although Pedro exiled him for his leadership of the opposition in the Constitutional Convention, in later years he could think of no one more suitable to be the tutor of his young son, the future Pedro II.

José Bonifacio de Andrada was born in Santos, State of São Paulo, Brazil, June 13, 1763. After preparatory studies in São Paulo, under Frei Manuel da Resurreição, he went to Portugal at the age of twenty to study in the University of Coimbra. For ten years, following his graduation, he traveled in Europe studying with the greatest scientists of the day: Lavoisier, de Chaptal, Jussíeu, Haüy, de Werner, Freislaben, Lempe and Lampadius. He became a member of many learned societies. He also showed himself a man of practical talents, when, during the Napoleonic invasion, he commanded an academic battalion in Portugal. Returning to Lisbon he continued to act as secretary of the Royal Academy of Science, and occupied several government posts, such as Inspector General of Mines. In the University of Coimbra he became Professor of Mineralogy.

When, in 1819, he arrived back home in Brazil, recalled by the Prince Regent, he was fifty-six years of age, a man of the world, and Brazil's outstanding man of knowledge. Refusing a ministerial appointment he retired to São Paulo. Here his presence was immediately felt, in the course of disturbances over acceptance of the new Portuguese Constitution. José Bonifacio restored order and as vice president of the Junta, became the real power in São Paulo. The Emperor, Pedro I, wrote (1821) to his father, João VI, now returned to Portugal, that the tranquility and security of São Paulo was in large measure due to José Bonifacio. Under his leadership in December 1821, the province took a strong stand urging the Prince Regent not to return to Portugal as the Portuguese Cortes was demanding. An alliance to prevent execution of the demands of the Cortes was arranged between São Paulo and Minas Geraes. This was the turning point. The prince agreed to resist the Portuguese demands.

On January 16, 1822, he made Andrada royal minister, although it was the Princess Leopoldina who notified him of the appointment. Andrada brought to Pedro the militant support of the Paulistas. More than any other Brazilian, he helped to organize Brazilian forces behind the Emperor Pedro and to support him in the imminent conflict with Portugal and the Portuguese party in Brazil. On August 6, 1822, he directed to the governments of friendly nations a manifesto which in many ways marks the beginning of the Brazilian nation. In it he explained the nature of Brazil's quarrel with Portugal, and the principles for which Brazil stood. The ports of Brazil, he wrote, would remain open to friendly nations for commerce and immigration. It was a declaration of independence without the formality of a break with Portugal, or with the Portuguese crown.

José Bonifacio saw and developed clearly the policy of independence. Desiring a complete rupture with Portugal he addressed Dom Pedro in a letter announcing the receipt of measures of refusal from Portugal, analyzing the situation and pointing out the necessity for a definitive step by the Prince. It was this letter which brought the Grito de Ipiranga, September 7, 1822: Pedro's declaration of "Independence or Death." With the capitulation of Jorge de Avilez at Playa Grande, Niterói, independence was practically assured. In quick succession an expedition was sent against Baía and a naval squadron was prepared under Lord Cochrane for the same purpose.

It was José Bonifacio who issued the call for a Constituent Assembly. At first, as minister, he defended the Emperor in the Assembly. He represented São Paulo provincial conservatism, aristocratic rural society, and "the monarchic ideal in its authoritarian, organic, unifying sense," [1] in opposition to the liberal urbanism and democratic tendencies of Rio de Janeiro. In defense of the Emperor he even resorted to stringent measures such as exiling the deputy, Feijó, a future regent. These conflicts brought the downfall of José Bonifacio's ministry on July 5, 1823.

With him went his brothers, Antonio Ribeiro, Minister of the Interior, and Martin Francisco, Minister of the Treasury, and his sister, Donna Maria Flora Ribeira de Andrada. Donna Maria, in the personal service of the Empress Leopoldina, had played a political role almost equal in importance to that of her brothers. After the departure of the Andradas the Emperor was forced to rely increasingly on the collaboration of the Portuguese and military elements in the country.

José Bonifacio entered the Constituent Assembly just in time to be involved in the heated conflict which developed over the new constitution. The crux of the argument was the veto power, although other liberal issues were also involved. He founded two newspapers to advance his liberal views on constitutional questions: *Tamoyo* in Rio de Janeiro, and *Sentinela de libertade*

---

[1] Calmon, *in* Levene, ed., *Historia de América* VIII, p.277.

á beira mar da Praia Grandé, in Pernambuco. Among the numerous proposals he supported at the time, two may be noted particularly: the establishment of a new capital city, Petropolis, and Christian education of the Indians. No other single individual had a greater influence in drafting the constitution.

Conflict between the Emperor and the Assembly over the Constitution brought the dissolution of the Assembly in 1823. José Bonifacio and his brothers were exiled. They were saved perhaps from a worse fate only by the personal intervention of George Canning and Ferdinand VII of Spain. His exile lasted six years, until 1829.

But there was to be one more chapter in José Bonifacio's long and eventful life. His formative influence on the Brazilian monarchy was not yet ended. In 1831, the Emperor, facing rebellion in Brazil and the prospect of complete loss of his Portuguese interests, abdicated in favor of his young seven-year-old son, the future Pedro II, and left Brazil to make himself the leader of Portuguese liberalism.

José Bonifacio was named royal tutor and for seven years, until his death in 1838, he was the center of the most turbulent politics in the whole history of Brazil, the politics of the so-called "republican" regency. Whether or not the Brazil of this period may be properly described as "republican," it is certainly true that the two regents elected during this period, Feijó and Araujo Lima, were republicans from the days of the Constitutional Assembly. José Bonifacio, identified with the interests of the young prince whom he was determined to educate in the principles of liberalism, was assailed from every side by partisans of both extremes. But he stood his ground and stuck to his task. As he had prepared the monarchy of Brazil for Dom Pedro I, he prepared Dom Pedro II for the liberal monarchy which followed the latter's accession to the throne in 1840.

Andrada e Silva, José Bonifacio de. O patriarcha da independencia, José Bonifacio de Andrada e Silva. (Bibliotheca Pedagogica Brasilera, Serie 5, v 166) Rio de Janeiro, Companhia Editora Nacional. 1939. 433p.

Calegoras, João Pandiá. A history of Brazil. Chapel Hill, University of North Carolina Press. 1939. p78-93, 120. (Ed. and tr. by Percy Alvin Martin).

Crane, John and Wilgus, A. C. José Bonifacio, the patriarch of Brazilian independence. Washington, American Patriot Series. 1942. 16p.

PART II

NINETEENTH CENTURY LIBERALS

The Generation of Sarmiento

It is too bad so much has been written by North Americans about the lack of Latin American political experience, for a great deal of such writing lies in the realm of dangerous half truth. To be sure, Latin Americans lacked experience with representative government on a national scale prior to their national independence. But a more significant lack was that of a large aggressive middle class with political experience. For while there were many Latin Americans experienced in the management of colonial affairs, and especially in local government, too often the most competent were identified with the traditional privileged class. The new mestizo leadership, pushing up to positions of power through the revolutionary armies, was inexperienced and untrained. All too frequently they found themselves at the mercy of the creoles who exploited them for their own purposes.

Frequently, too, mestizo leaders proved irresponsible in positions of authority, lending themselves to arbitrary excesses of the worst sort. This tended to be particularly true in countries with large Indian populations, in which the mestizos, in a certain sense, stood between the creoles and the Indian (or sometimes Negro) masses. In general, this is the explanation of the terrible Carerra dictatorship in Guatemala, of Melgarejo in Bolivia, and of a number of others which might be cited. In any case, if Hispanic Americans lacked political experience prior to independence, the nineteenth century brought them the most varied experience in organizing democratic political structures in the face of the greatest difficulties.

Their new states were basically weak because, as conscious political entities, they depended so largely upon the creole leadership in the movement for independence and that of the few mestizos who had been drawn into active political participation on a national scale. The vast majority of the Indian and mestizo population were left untouched by the new nation state. Living in a subsistence economy, with a social outlook and attitudes like those of the medieval European peasantry, they centered their lives and their attention around the local village community, their *tierra*.

The new states were weak, also, because the European conquest was not yet complete in the sense of cultural and racial assimilation, and a great social and psychological schism persisted in the separation of the conquerors from the conquered. They were weak because of lack of adequate national revenues, and because defaulted debts in many cases seriously impaired national credit. At the beginning of the nineteenth century, none of the states could boast a national commerce thriving enough to provide tax revenue sufficient to maintain an adequate army or police force. In many states early reform plans had created deep-seated disagreements with the Church. Church and State, all too frequently, instead of offering mutual aid and support in the task of building the new national social and political order, wasted each other's strength in conflict. Finally, these new states were weak because the long drawn out struggle for independence left them with the incubus of a system of militarism in which real political power was open to any petty local leader able to command the services of a band of personal followers.

Nineteenth century liberal leadership in Latin America thus faced a baffling combination of circumstances: deep-cut lines of racial and cultural division, widespread illiteracy, lack of national consciousness on the part of large sectors of the population, militarism and caudillism inherited from the wars of independence, general and widespread poverty, inadequate national revenues, an unsound land system which concentrated ownership in the hands of a small minority, plus deep-seated traditionalism in the creole class which owned the land and dominated the church. Perhaps one must ascribe it to New World optimism that a group of liberal leaders was able to face all these difficulties with any degree of confidence that their reforms would lay the social basis for a stable, orderly and free political system.

Their ideas were very much those of liberals elsewhere during the nineteenth century, characterized by over optimism and confidence in overly simple solutions. They hoped to liberate the individual from tyranny, superstition and oppression, and to liberate his abilities by education. Their simple solution of all their national ills was to liberate the wealth in the hands of the Church, liberate the Indians and Negroes from the feudal land and labor systems in which they were held, rid their lands of Spanish and Portuguese influence, provide for general education, encourage the immigration of non-Hispanic people, culture and capital by favorable laws, and develop systems of transportation, commerce and industry by encouraging free enterprise. That this could all be done quickly they were confident, because they saw how quickly it was being done in the United States.

But the task of inaugurating a new era of free and expanding economic activity was much more formidable in Latin America than in the United States. In Latin America it had to be performed in the midst of political and social anarchy and disorganization, performed, they felt, before that anarchy could give way to order and prosperity. To many of us today the faith of these liberals in their simple plans for reform seems very naive. We see that they failed to understand racial and population problems and tendencies of their times, underestimated the importance of the church question and of religious factors in general, and failed to make proper allowance for the persistence of traditional forces in society. But that, of course, is because we have seen their failures in historical perspective.

In Argentina, the generation of San Martín and Rivadavia had failed to achieve a permanent and stable Argentine union because of the magnitude of the task they had undertaken and of the forces they had loosed. San Martín, after the failure of his scheme for liberal monarchy, had retired to Europe in unhappy, self-imposed exile, forgotten by his countrymen. Rivadavia, brilliant even in the failure of his plans for an enlightened, progressive, centralized Argentina, had seen all his reforms crumble with the overthrow of the shaky political structure upon which he had erected them, and had followed San Martín to Europe.

Yet, out of the very darkness of this failure came the generation of Sarmiento, Alberdi, Mitre and Avellaneda, the greatest Argentina has produced, perhaps the greatest group of leaders in Latin American history. Growing up amid the enthusiasm of the early days of independence, they were just entering politics as young men in the disastrous days following the overthrow of Rivadavia, and during the years when the sinister shadow of Juan Manuel Rosas was spreading over the land. They were just old enough to be fired with enthusiasm for the plans of Rivadavia. But neither they nor their country, apparently, had had enough of the bitter hard experience, of the trials and difficulties of building a constitutional regime from the refractory materials of the sparsely populated pampas and their half savage, mestizo gauchos to know how to prevent the Rosas dictatorship.

One by one they got into trouble with the dictator and traveled the road to exile. That is, all except Avellaneda, who paid with his life the price of his premature leadership of his native province in a program of reform. Sarmiento, Alberdi and Mitre pondered the causes of their country's anarchy and dictatorship during long years of exile. They analyzed the social causes of the political failure and gave to Argentina and to Latin America their first political philosophy.

Bartolomé Mitre became the mainstay of Buenos Aires after the overthrow of Rosas, and the realistic, practical, political and military leader in the subsequent struggle of Buenos Aires with Urquiza and the federation of the other Argentine provinces. He became the first real president of a united Argentina, as well as the indefatigable historian of his country's political vicissitudes. Alberdi was the Madison of the group. His alert and realistic intelligence contributed the diagnosis of the political situation which was adopted by Urquiza and the other leaders against Rosas as the basis of the Constitution of 1853. Domingo F. Sarmiento was the insistent voice of the Argentine conscience. It was the voice of a schoolmaster to two nations, teaching them the nature of the problems they had to solve, and pointing out with confidence the road to their solution.

Although no other Latin American state can rival this galaxy of great names, almost every one produced at least one liberal leader of this type. In

Chile it was Manuel Montt, and, later, Balmaceda; in Peru, Castilla and González Prada; in Guatemala, Rufino Barrios; in Mexico, Benito Juárez. The failures of this generation of liberal leadership were great, as were their successes. But their failures should not be judged too harshly. We can see now that they had to fail in many respects. Yet they won notable victories, too, in Argentina, Brazil, Chile, Mexico, and Peru, as will appear in the sketches which follow. Their shortcomings were partly those of their age, and partly the result of the extremely difficult conditions under which they worked.

Tragic as their individual lives often were, they achieved remarkable results in the form of political stability and, with it, economic prosperity in Latin America. With their passing Latin America remained for another generation without political leadership of this heroic, idealistic type. Not until after World War I did another such confident, optimistic generation arise.

Juan Bautista Alberdi (1810-1884)

Citizen of Solitude

The Revolution of 1810 marked the real beginning of independence in Argentina and the Congress of Tucumán in 1816 rallied the Argentine provinces to a formal break in the ties to Spain. Yet the leaders of this early period in Argentine history failed signally in the task of providing a workable constitution and political stability for the struggling, disunited and sparsely populated provinces of the Plate River valley. The result was thirty years of civil war, internal disorder, and the personal dictatorship of Juan Manuel Rosas—the darkest period in the history of the Argentine nation, and all the darker because of the bright prospects with which Argentine independence began. Many of the early leaders, like Dorrego, paid for this failure with their lives. Others, like San Martín, Rivadavia and Lavalle, retired to lonely and bitter exile. Yet out of the very darkness of their failure came a new generation who were to succeed where their fathers had failed. Bartolomé Mitre, Domingo F. Sarmiento, Nicolás Avellaneda, Juan Bautista Alberdi and their generation were children too young to participate in the movement for independence. Their childhood was lived in the invigorating atmosphere of the new liberation, but their youth encountered the fratricidal strife, the discouraging social and political anarchy, and the cynical and primitive rule of force of the Mazorca and gaucho-caudillo dictatorship of Juan Manuel Rosas.

In the crucible of these agonizing years the spirit of this new generation was tempered, each in his own way, into the fine hard instruments which rescued Argentina from its initial failures, and laid the basis for its later development. Avellaneda paid the price of a brilliant but premature leadership of reform with his life. Mitre became the realistic, practical military and political leader, and the first real president of the united nation. Sarmiento was the apocalyptical voice of judgment, thundering from his exile in Chile across the Andes, a voice which the forces of despotism were powerless to still or to combat. But Sarmiento could not conceive of thought divorced from action. In the realm of practical politics he played a part fully proportionate to his role of writer, and his presidential administration was the most prolific in basic measures and accomplishments for the future nation in all its history.

The figure of Juan Bautista Alberdi is in striking contrast. He was a failure in politics, except for two brilliant successes as the diplomatic representative of the government of Urquiza in Europe, where he secured the long overdue recognition of Argentine independence by Spain, and the recognition of Urquiza's government as the legitimate government of the federation. His brief return to his native country to serve in the Congress after 1880, was a complete failure and soon brought him to seek another self-imposed exile in France. He had become a stranger in his own country! His most recent biographer, the Argentine Pablo Rojas Paz, characterizes him aptly as a "citizen of solitude," whose efforts to influence the destinies of his country by pure thought began by alienating him from his former collaborators, and brought him finally to the place where he could neither understand nor be understood by his own countrymen.

He was born in 1810 in Tucumán, western Argentina, just three years before Belgrano's great victory over the Spanish forces in that place, and six years before the even more famous Congress which declared Argentine independence. His father, Salvador Alberdi, one of the leaders in the cause of independence, had been declared an honorary citizen of the Provinces of La Plata by the Congress of Tucumán. His older brother likewise played an important role in the early government. But independence was an accomplished fact by the time the now orphaned Juan Bautista, at the age of fifteen, made the sixty-day journey with a train of oxcarts to Buenos Aires to complete his education. There he witnessed the series of events which brought the Rosas dictatorship. He was, in fact, patronized by several of the leaders of this regime, even to the extent of a commission from the noted Quiroga to travel and study in the United States, a commission which he refused at the last moment on grounds of conscience. Sympathy with opponents of Rosas led him to become a member of the literary salon of Marcos Sastre, where he was associated with Juan María Gutiérrez, Mármol, Vicente Fidel López and Echeverría. Soon he joined the colony of refugees in Montevideo, and when Rosas began the siege of that place, escaped to Paris. This first period of his exile in Paris is important chiefly because it gave him the breadth of experience which enabled him later to write his famous *Bases . . . for the Political Organization of the Argentine Republic.*

Much has been written about this famous book. No other Argentine book has been more discussed. Yet it was written hurriedly, to meet the situation created by the overthrow of Rosas. Perhaps the most important fact was that it won the approval of General Urquiza, leader of the anti-Rosas forces, whose great prestige was chiefly responsible for the acceptance of its proposals by the constitutional congress in 1853. Alberdi, because of this book, has rightfully been called the father of the Argentine constitution. Certainly it is the nearest thing in Latin American political literature to the *Federalist Papers* or John Adams' famous *Defense of the American Constitutions* in our own. Like them, it is characterized by a keen sense of political realities, and of the necessity of searching for the basis of a constitution in existing governmental institutions and of making realistic compromises to protect the interests of the other provinces against the overwhelming influence of the province of Buenos Aires.

His criticism of the conduct of the allied nations in the war against Paraguay brought Alberdi a great deal of criticism in Argentina. A few years before his death he returned to Argentina briefly to become a member of Congress, only to find himself the center of bitter and personal controversy. A year or so later, he returned to France a sad and disillusioned man. He died in Paris in 1884 a lonely exile, leaving as his greatest contribution a book which had laid the constitutional basis of a great nation.

Alberdi, Juan B.   Bases y puntos de partida para la organización política de la República Argentina.   Buenos Aires, Talleres Graficos Argentinos, L. J. Rosso.   1933.   323p.   (Ed. by Francisco Cruz).

Crawford, W. Rex.   A century of Latin-American thought.   Cambridge, Mass., Harvard University Press.   1944.   p18-37.

Mijares, Augusto.   Hombres e ideas en América.   Caracas, Escuela Técnica Industrial.   1940.   p29-50.

Quesada, Ernesto.   La figura histórica de Alberdi.   2nd ed.   Buenos Aires, Imprenta Schenone.   1919.   42p.

Rojas Paz, Pablo.   Alberdi, el ciudadano de la soledad.   Buenos Aires, Losada.   1941.   315p.

Domingo Faustino Sarmiento (1811-1888)

School Teacher to a Nation

Augusto Mijares of Venezuela has recently pointed out that Argentina's mid-nineteenth century generation of Alberdi, Sarmiento and Mitre was probably the greatest in the literary, cultural and educational history of Latin America, yet, that outside Argentina they are known today only by name, or for the official positions they held.[1]

Pondering in unhappy exile the political and social chaos and dictatorship which succeeded Argentine independence, Mitre, Alberdi and Sarmiento discovered its latent social causes, and evolved a social and political philosophy—a sense of direction—the first of its kind in Latin America. Explaining the nature of the political and social phenomena which bred political disorder they taught America a lesson still valid in many respects today, and too little known.

Alberdi's ideas have just been noted. Let us now turn to the greatest of this group, Domingo F. Sarmiento, the "complete man," school teacher, revolutionist, historian, president, founder of the school system of Argentina, the man who gave Argentina its greatest presidential administration and more than any other single individual established its political stability as a government not of men but of laws.

He was born February 14, 1811 in San Juan, capital of the western Andean province of San Juan in Argentina. Although his parents were poor, his mother came from the formerly wealthy de Oro family, who held prominent church and government positions in San Juan and neighboring provinces, and had taken active part in the movement for Argentine independence. His father was a muleteer in the army for the liberation of Chile, which the great San Martín had recruited in this region. Domingo had been too young to take an active part in the war, but the impression made upon his young mind by San Martín and the Army of Liberation was one which would never be erased.

Domingo grew up in a time of great political chaos lasting from the Declaration of Argentine Independence in 1816, through the Rosas dictatorship which began in 1829 and lasted until 1852. During these years all efforts to achieve a stable federal union and constitution, even Rosas' rule of iron in Buenos Aires, failed. The rivalries of the military caudillos who ruled the provinces, the jealousy of Buenos Aires on the part of the provinces

[1] Mijares, Augusto. *Hombres e ideas en América*, Caracas, Escuela Técnica Industrial. 1940. p.19-21.

which were dominated by colonialism and the spirit of the gaucho, and the constant threat of intervention presented by a complicated international situation involving France, Great Britain, Brazil, Paraguay and Uruguay, all contributed to this failure.

Sarmiento was a precocious boy, the outstanding student in the new revolutionary school established in San Juan, and his parents, poverty stricken though they were, were determined he should have a good education. For a while their plans seemed to come to grief when local politics kept Domingo from a deserved scholarship for study in Buenos Aires. He went, instead, to study with an uncle, a priest who had been banished to the isolated mountain community of San Francisco del Monte. Here he also taught his first school of a few Indians and mestizos.

Committed to the cause of national unity, so brilliantly and disastrously defended in Buenos Aires by Rivadavia, Sarmiento and the group of young unitarians [2] in San Juan soon came into conflict with the federalist governor established in the province by Rosas. An orgy of beheadings followed,. but luckily he escaped from San Juan with his life. The next years, until 1858, were spent in exile in Chile.

There he made the friendship of the great Manuel Montt, who encouraged him in his journalistic and educational interests. Sarmiento's gift for journalism here showed itself. He edited several newspapers, conducted a campaign for general education, and, at Montt's instance, drafted the law which founded the Chilean elementary school system. His powerful pen made him the leader of the Argentine exiles in Chile who were devoted to the overthrow of Rosas.

Among his writings, his *Facundo,* published in 1845, is especially important. It is a study of the great gaucho leader and friend of Rosas, Facundo Quiroga. It is also a social and political philosophy. Facundo represented the barbarism of the ranchers and mestizo plainsmen of the pampas which opposed law and order in an exaggerated notion of individual freedom. The dictator had established his power on the basis of this force, wrote Sarmiento, and this power could not be broken until intelligent unitarians and federalists united to suppress the barbarism of the pampas with law and order. Travel in Europe and the United States, where he formed a life-long friendship with Horace Mann and Mrs. Mann, also convinced him that the nations of America must find their own salvation, not copy that of Europe, and that they could rise to their destiny only through a great educational crusade.

It was a union of the kind Sarmiento proposed, the union led by Urquiza, governor of Entre Rios, which overthrew Rosas in 1852. But

[2] The followers of Rivadavia advocated a unitary state.

Sarmiento soon broke with Urquiza because he felt Urquiza was trying to establish his personal rule. Again in exile in Chile, he engaged in a great political argument with Alberdi, new minister of the Argentine Confederation in Chile. Alberdi's *Bases y puntos de partida* was the basis of the Constitution of 1853 imposed by Urquiza and a group of provincial governors. Alberdi defended the policies of Urquiza while Sarmiento urged a closer union of the provinces with Buenos Aires based on a constitution freely arrived at.

In 1858, after his friend Mitre had become governor of Buenos Aires, Sarmiento returned to Argentina, and began at once to take an active part in affairs. At first, as minister of education in Buenos Aires he initiated a program of public education. Then he was elected governor of his native province of San Juan, and gave it a model administration, founding schools, paving streets, and suppressing lawlessness and disorder. In the meantime he had taken a prominent part in the constitutional convention which brought Buenos Aires back into the Confederation. From 1864 to 1868 he was the Argentine minister in Washington, renewing old acquaintances, and increasing his respect and liking for the United States public schools and for her constitution.

Elected President of Argentina in 1868, while he was serving as minister in Washington, he gave his country its greatest and most progressive administration. He vigorously suppressed insurrections which threatened to undo the work of pacification of the leaders of 1852. At the conclusion of the Paraguayan War, he prevented partition of Paraguay, saying, "Victory gives no rights." He founded schools and urged taxes for their public support, created the national bank, reformed the criminal code, secured adoption of a new commercial code and law of weights and measures, fostered the building of roads, railroads, telegraph lines, and the international cable, reformed the army, founded the modern Argentine navy, founded the astronomical observatory at Córdoba and established the Argentine postal service on a solid basis. The first national census was taken under his administration.

Throughout his administration, moreover, he fought stubbornly but unsuccessfully to break up the system of large land holdings in favor of small owners. Land reform and the elimination of ignorance by free public education, likewise realized only in part, were the two measures he saw as most necessary to cure the conditions which produced the constant revolutions and political anarchy of Latin America.

After his presidency he served for a time as senator from San Juan, and for several years directed the schools, first of the Province of Buenos Aires, and later of the nation. His enormous energy was poured out in favor of education, the suppression of disorder, and measures for economic advance, in books, in articles, and in the newspaper, *La Nacional*, which he edited for a time. He was a crusader to his death on September 11, 1888, and his fifty volumes of works, published by the Argentine government, are not only a great contribution to Argentine literature, but an incomparable legacy of political, educational and social doctrine. A great intellect constantly devoted to the redemption and development of his country and proud of the title of schoolmaster, he lived his dictum that "to govern is to educate," and proved to be the rare example of a man of great learning, who was also great in the administration of practical affairs, Argentina's "complete man."

Crawford, W. Rex. A century of Latin-American thought. Cambridge, Mass., Harvard University Press. 1944. p37-51.

Galván Moreno, C. Radiografía de Sarmiento. Buenos Aires, Claridad. 1938. 499p.

Lugones, Leopoldo. Historia de Sarmiento, Buenos Aires, 1911. Selection in English translation *in* Arciniegas, Germán, ed. The green continent. New York, Knopf. 1944. p337-54.

Mijares, Augusto. Hombres e ideas en América. Caracas, Escuela Técnica Industrial. 1940. p19-28, 41-50.

Nichols, Madaline W. Sarmiento: a chronicle of Inter-American friendship. Washington, The author. 1940. 81p. Bibliography.

Watt, Stewart and Peterson, H. F. Builders of Latin America. New York, Harper & Brothers. 1942. Chapter 17.

BARTOLOMÉ MITRE (1821-1906)

Soldier, Artisan of Argentine Union, and Historian

Bartomomé Mitre is the later day exponent of the spirit of liberal reform which had characterized Buenos Aires in the days following the May (1810) Revolution—sobered, hardened, and turned realistic by the bitter frustration of decades of political instability. Tall, dark, military in bearing, keenly intelligent, in every sense a man of the world, he was for Buenos Aires and the new Argentine nation which emerged after 1852, what Urquiza was for the provinces and the renewed Confederation of 1852-53. There is a long argument, still unsettled in Argentina, over the relations of Urquiza and Mitre to each other and their relative roles in fashioning the Argentine Union. No student of Argentine history can refuse to either of them, however, a place among the great founders of the nation, those "unknown vital forces" of liberalism which Augusto Mijares has described as awaiting, during the Rosas dictatorship, the propitious moment to form and establish civil political union and stability.[1] To many indeed, Mitre is more than just one of this group; he is indisputably the foremost among the architects of the Argentine nation.

By 1850, Juan Manuel de Rosas could no longer justify his dictatorship of Argentina upon the basis of internal anarchy and foreign wars, and it was becoming increasingly difficult for him to defend his failure to establish the long promised constitution. His attempt to provoke a quarrel with Paraguay in 1852 brought the uprising of the governor of Entre Rios, Urquiza, and his constitutionalist followers.

After overthrowing Rosas, Urquiza followed the general plan set forth in Alberdi's *Bases*. Having first secured the agreement of the governors of the provinces at San Nicolás, he led in the reestablishment of the Confederation under a new constitution drawn up by representatives of all the provinces except Buenos Aires, and became the first president under the new constitution. Under the leadership of Governor Alsina and Mitre, however, Buenos Aires remained away from the constitutional convention and stayed outside the Confederation until 1826. Mitre's argument was that the agreement of San Nicolás, under which the convention met, would really establish the despotic rule of Urquiza and the province of Entre Rios. Other questions were also involved, of course, such as the provinces' jealousy and fear of the province of Buenos Aires, the latter's monopoly of foreign trade and the

[1] Mijares, Augusto. *Interpretación pesimista de la sociología hispano americana.* Caracas, Coop. de Artes Gráficas. 1938. 83p.

revenues from import taxes, her interest in liberalized tariff laws and other liberal reforms which frightened the more conservative provinces, and her control of foreign relations, which she had become accustomed to exercising for the other provinces. But Mitre led the attack when the constitution was being discussed in the Buenos Aires Congress, upon the basis of the threat of dictatorship by Urquiza. Because of his leadership, and because of Urquiza's forbearance, Buenos Aires was able to stay out of the Confederation for a decade.

Mitre's great genius as soldier-statesman in the consolidation of the Argentine union then appears in his bringing Buenos Aires back into the Confederation. This he did, first, under a compromise plan adopted after the drawn battle of Cepeda (1859), which unfortunately, settled none of the issues. The union was accomplished definitively, after his triumph over the forces of the Confederation in the Battle of Pavón (1861), and Mitre was then elected president. Argentina now held her first truly national congress, political anarchy came to an end, and the country began its uninterrupted political and economic progress as a nation.[2]

Bartolomé Mitre was born June 26, 1821, in Buenos Aires. Like many boys of his day, his early education was provided by tutors in his home, and by his father. His early childhood, like that of Alberdi and Sarmiento, was spent in the invigorating atmosphere of the newly won independence. His youth, like theirs, encountered bitter partisan strife, anarchy, and finally the desperate frustration of the Rosas dictatorship. Mitre was the youngest of a group of ardent liberals who fled to Montevideo, "to fight for the banner of May" (the May 1810 uprising), not to return except to join Urquiza in the revolt culminating in the Battle of Caseros in 1852.

In Montevideo, in 1836-37, he studied in the Academia Militar. By 1838, he had received the rank of captain and was launched on a military career, which soon brought him the rank of lieutenant colonel. During the long siege of Montevideo by the forces of General Oribe he took an active part in the defense. Here, too, during the first year of the siege he met and later married the charming young Delfina de Vedia, daughter of a general in the Uruguayan army.

The second period of Mitre's exile centers in Bolivia. Here he served under President Ballivián with great distinction as Director of the Military College, and in various military engagements. The last year of his exile was spent in Santiago, Chile, a member of the distinguished group of Argentinians then contributing to the literary and educational activities of the Chilean metropolis. It was at this time, through his writing for *El Mercurio*, that he first became a literary rival of Domingo Faustino Sarmiento.

---

[2] This view of Mitre's importance is not without contradiction by Argentine historians. See especially Julio Victorica, *Urquiza y Mitre*, Buenos Aires, 1918.

The director of *El Mercurio* was Felix Vicuña, father of Benjamín Vicuña Mackenna, the great Chilean historian, with whom Mitre now began a lifelong friendship. His Santiago days also marked the beginning of a strong but platonic attachment to another of the Vicuña clan, Eugenia Vicuña de Rodríguez Peña, wife of the son of one of the Argentina liberators. In the romantic temper of his times he wrote poems to express his love and esteem for this charming woman. The extent of his feeling was shown years later when he was called upon to be godfather and to name the newly born daughter of his friend Vicuña Mackenna. He named her Eugenia, saying, "May you be like the other of your name . . . all intelligence, all beauty, all goodness, all virtue. . . . May there always be a Eugenia Vicuña in Chile." [3]

Mitre joined the other Argentine exiles in the Urquiza uprising and fought at the side of the great caudillo in the battle of Caseros which brought the downfall of Rosas in 1852. But from that point on the paths of the two separated. Urquiza, as president of the Confederation was the undisputed political leader of the provinces, while Mitre, as already pointed out, identified himself more with the city and province of Buenos Aires. Yet one may well note one respect, at least, in which the two were playing comparable roles. Both symbolized the underlying forces that made for Argentine stability, and the strength of their leadership lay in this fact. Urquiza was the caudillo who had learned to subordinate personal power to the cause of union, and who, by the prestige of his example and the intelligence of his policies as president, imposed this principle upon the other caudillo governors. Mitre, equally committed to the principle of burying the partisan animosities which had led Argentina into political chaos, represented the city, the metropolis. He was the realistic statesman and soldier. He was able to see and forge the practical means by which the economic and social measures urged by the liberals of Buenos Aires could be achieved in conjunction with the entrance of Buenos Aires into the Confederation.

As president, after 1862, he moved slowly and cautiously against the power of the caudillos who still dominated the provinces. Gradually the liberal system of free trade was spread over the nation. Immigration increased, and the first steps toward railroad building were taken. Mitre's greatest task as president, however, was to lead the nation in its war against Paraguay.

The war originated in a conflict between Paraguay and Brazil and was never popular in Argentina. Mitre had tried for a while to steer a neutral course. The issue was taken out of his hands, however, when President López of Paraguay determined to lead his troops across Argentine soil to attack the Brazilians in Uruguay. Argentina immediately joined with Brazil and

---

[3] Niño, José M. *Mitre, su vida íntima, histórica, hechos, reminiscencias, episodios y anécdotas militares y civiles.* Buenos Aires, Ad. Grau. 1906. v2, p89.

the party of Flores in Uruguay in a triple alliance. There were those who, like Alberdi, felt the war was never justified. Mitre was convinced, however, that to remain out was either to encourage increased Brazilian intervention in La Plata affairs, or the dominance of Argentina by López of Paraguay. The air was clarified somewhat by Urquiza's endorsement and support of the war. However, the struggle dragged out its long, bitter course, to the death of López on the battlefield. Mitre was increasingly away with the army, pre-occupied with military affairs as the allied commander, and out of touch with developments at home.

Sarmiento, his former literary rival, was elected president in 1868. The election was a three cornered contest, one in which Mitre was chiefly trying to defeat Urquiza. As a result the candidate he was himself supporting was defeated by Sarmiento.

Mitre was only forty-seven at the time and a long life of usefulness still lay before him. Entering the congress as senator from Buenos Aires, he became the acknowledged leader of the opposition to Sarmiento, especially after Sarmiento came to an understanding with Urquiza. Mitre's newspaper, La Nación, rivaled La Tribuna as a national organ of political opinion, and became a powerful political instrument in his hands. He continued active in Argentine politics for the next three decades. Twice, in 1874 and 1880, he tried unsuccessfully to intervene in presidential elections. Yet even these failures had great effect in national political life, and Mitre's prestige and popularity always stood as a solid rock against perpetuation in office and caudillism. Even in defeat he was powerful. In 1874, he headed an armed uprising in protest against a controlled election. He was quickly defeated and made prisoner, yet when he was brought as a captive to the town of Lujan he was still so much the idol of the people, that they turned out en masse to acclaim him.

Later years found him increasingly absorbed in historical studies. In 1888, he published his History of Belgrano and in 1889 his San Martín. These two works have had a great influence on the study of Latin American history, and are still considered basic works. For the latter he made a special trip to Chile to trace out the military campaigns of the great leader of independence, and incidentally, to revisit the scene of his own exile. His literary activity alone during these years, including archeological, historical, linguistic, literary and military studies, is enough to constitute a life's work of great distinction, entirely aside from his political activities.

Returning from a trip to Europe in 1890, he was greeted with a gala reception by friends and followers, both in Montevideo and Buenos Aires. Yet this reception, great as it was, did not begin to equal the celebration of his eightieth birthday, in 1901, when a national feriada of several days was declared in his honor. When in 1902, he resigned from the senate, it was to terminate an active political career of more than three score years. Four years later, at the time of his death, he received the most elaborate ceremony of recognition ever given an Argentine statesman!

His record is unique in respect to his long period of useful active life following his retirement from the presidency. From 1868 to 1906 he was his country's first citizen. So active was he in national affairs of all kinds that it may be safely said his influence and achievements during these years actually outweigh those of his presidency. Of the United States presidents, only John Quincy Adams would seem to rival Mitre's record, and Adams scarcely equalled Mitre in his continuing popularity. Nor was Adams in the same peculiar sense the founder of his nation, living on through long years to see the fruits, derived peculiarly from his rule, show themselves in continuously expanding national stability and prosperity. For, when all due allowance had been made for Mitre's illustrious predecessors and successors, it was his peculiar privilege to forge the real and lasting Argentine union out of the elements brought into being by the Revolution of 1852.

Melián Lafinur, Álvaro. Figuras Americanas. Paris, Casa Editorial Franco-Ibero-Americana. 1926. p105-11.

Niño, José M. Mitre, su vida íntima, histórica, hechos, reminiscencias, episodios y anécdotas militares y civiles. Buenos Aires, Imprenta y Casa Editora de Ad. Grau. 1906. 2v.

Victorica, Julio. Urquiza y Mitre, con una introducción de Julio Barreda Lynch. Buenos Aires, La Cultura Argentina. 1918. 607p.

DIEGO JOSÉ VÍCTOR PORTALES (1793-1837)

The Strong Man of Chile

The colossal figure of Diego Portales, a century after his death, recently hovered again over Chilean politics. Pro-Fascist opponents of the leftist National Front in the late nineteen thirties made a cult of him. They described him as the great strong man of the early years of Chilean independence who established discipline, law and order, and thus laid the solid basis upon which later national prosperity could be built. On the other side, the National Front, consisting of Socialists, Communists, middle-class radicals, and labor union representatives, depreciated his historical position although he has long been considered the father of his country and of the Constitution of 1833—the man principally responsible for establishing the political stability of Chile. Reacting against their Fascist enemies they pictured him as the representative of a reactionary, land-owning oligarchy, opposed to all the new currents of liberalism produced by the movement for Chilean independence, and interested only in restoring the old colonialism of the eighteenth century. Instead of being the founder of his country, they suggested he was merely the founder of a political system which concentrated power in the hands of an oligarchy of wealth and which stood in the way of liberal reform for a century.

The real Portales was neither of these extremes, although he had some of the character of both. In the final analysis he was a conservative, and some readers may feel that on this account he does not appropriately belong among the makers of democracy in Latin America. However, it is well to recall that democracy has needed, and continues to need, conservative leadership under certain circumstances. Portales' career in Chile is probably an illustration. It suggests certain analogies to that of Vasconcellos in Brazil.

Diego José Víctor Portales was descended from a colonial family whose ancestral tree included the evil and eccentric figure of La Quintrala, a woman whose name became a by-word in Chile for her extreme cruelty to her slaves and vindictive anger to others. Even after her death she was thought by simple superstitious folk to haunt the countryside as an evil spirit. Diego was born in Santiago de Chile on June 16, 1793, when the four-year-old French Revolution was just entering the radical stage of the Terror, and a year before the conservative Thermidorian Reaction, displacing the radicals, gave the Revolution stability and a constitution. There is a certain historical symbolism in this fact. This Chilean boy, born in the fateful year of 1793, before the force of the French Revolution had made itself fully felt in Latin America, would grow up to become the businessman leader of a similar conservative reaction in his native Chile against the liberal reform tendencies of the early leaders of the independence movement.

He was educated in the Colegio de San Carlos of Santiago. Since he never attended the University he always, in later years, had a certain feeling of inferiority in the presence of other Chilean leaders of superior education and social position. At an early age he was employed in the mint, but soon left to enter commerce. By the time of the war for independence he was a prosperous *estanquero*, dealing in official monopolies. Though he seems to have favored the revolutionary cause, he took little active part in the military movement which established Chilean independence in 1818. During the years that followed, under the rule of O'Higgins and of General Freire who supplanted O'Higgins' liberal reforming regime by force in 1823, civil war and partisan rivalry were the rule for nearly six years. It was at this juncture that Portales emerged as the efficient organizer of the Pelucones, or "Big Wigs." The Pelucones were the conservatives who feared O'Higgins' liberal reforms and the demogogic tendencies of the Pipiolos, or "Greenhorns," led by General Freire. The defeat of the Pipiolos by the Pelucones came in large measure as a result of Portales' work of organization. Although he was not its author in a literary sense, the Constitution of 1833, under which Chile was to be governed for nearly a century, was largely his handiwork.

But Portales preferred being the strong man behind the scenes to being the ruler. It was due to his influence, in a considerable degree, that Chile elected Joaquín Prieto, the first of a series of three strong conservative presidents who were each to rule for two five-year terms, during the next three decades.

Portales himself became Minister of the Interior, Foreign Relations, and War, keeping the reins of power well in his hands at first. In 1832 immediately after the defeat of the Pipiolos, he resigned to become governor of the turbulent port of Valparaiso. In four months he had reorganized the city and reformed conditions completely, restoring peace and order in a port city which the rapidly growing whaling and China trade had given the reputation of being one of the most lawless in the continent. While there he also established the naval school of Valparaiso, thus laying the foundation for the important Chilean navy and merchant marine.

He thought his job was completed and retired to private life. In 1835, however, he was recalled by President Prieto to end the partisan discord and civil disorder which had arisen in the country. Again he became Minister of Interior, War, and Foreign Relations, organizing the nation to meet the threat of an invading expedition headed by former president Freire. Freire enjoyed the support of the Bolivian dictator, Santa Cruz, who had recently made himself "Protector" of united Bolivia and Peru. The defeat and capture of Freire, a great military hero of the War for Independence, was a brilliant and almost unexpected success.

Feeling that the union of Peru and Bolivia threatened to absorb Chile, Portales next turned his attention to organizing a war to unseat the dictator, Santa Cruz. In 1837 he was assassinated while in the midst of the preparations for this war. A part of the military expedition assembled for the war against Peru mutinied and captured him while he was reviewing troops. The mutineers marched on Santiago, carrying Portales in chains, and when they saw that their defeat was certain, shot him. In spite of Portales' assassination, Chile was successful in the war, and Santa Cruz was driven from Bolivia.

Portales was never a man to engender affection or loyalty, but was always feared and hated even by many who supported him loyally because of his great ability, political astuteness and complete integrity. Yet one should not be blinded to his real qualities by the truculent and somewhat sinister character with which politically inspired controversy has invested him. Under his tutelage Chile became the first of the Spanish American republics to achieve stability. He set the example of a strong man of complete integrity, who refused to grasp the supreme power but was content to work in the background, and thus gave to Latin America one of its most important lessons in political leadership.

Encina, Francisco A. Portales; introducción a la historia de la época de Diego Portales (1830-1891). Santiago, Nascimento. 1934. 2v.

Galdames, Luis. History of Chile. (Inter-American history series, v4) Chapel Hill, University of North Carolina Press. 1941. p236-7, 261-70, 507-8, et passim. (Ed. and tr. by Isaac Joslin Cox).

Soto Hall, Máximo. Don Diego Portales. (Historia novelada) Santiago de Chile, Claridad. 1935. 202p.

Wilgus, A. Curtis, ed. South American dictators during the first century of independence. (Studies in Hispanic American affairs, v5) Washington, George Washington University Press. 1937. 510p. Ch. 13· "Diego Portales, dictator and organizer of Chile."

FRANCISCO MORAZÁN (1793-1842)

Martyr to Central American Union

With the death of Francisco Morazán in 1842 died the best hope that a strong and united nation would arise in the American isthmus on the basis of the old Guatemalan Captaincy General of the Spanish Empire in America. With Morazán, too, died the best hope of early liberal democracy in that region. A dark cloud of reactionary petty localism and militarism settled over the land from Chiapas to Costa Rica, to be lifted only briefly here and there, during the century which followed, by liberal regimes like that of Rufino Barrios in Guatemala. It was a cloud which was to make Central American dictatorship and militarism bywords in Latin America.

Not that the annals of the Central American states are lacking in other brave figures of liberal outlook. The peculiar glory of Latin American liberalism has been the relentless daring with which men of liberal views, even when they knew such opposition was hopeless, have opposed the impossible and petty tyrannies under which they lived. Such Central Americans as Matías Delgado, Rufino Barrios, José del Valle and Mariano Gálvez are deserving of a high place in anyone's annals of the great liberal age of democracy. Yet Morazán towers over them like a Jefferson or a Jackson in the United States.

Of course he was ahead of his times, trying to give to his people a society based upon general education, religious liberty and social and political equality for which they were not prepared, either by their history or their economic organization. Like his contemporary, Gómez Farías in Mexico, he saw the liberal reform in too simple terms: public schools, disestablishment of the Church, federal union, liberty of speech and the press, and liberal recodification of laws. Impatient for immediate reform, he failed to allow for the unreadiness of the creole and mestizo masses of his countrymen for such institutions, just as he failed to allow sufficiently for the shortsighted opposition by forces of petty reaction to any measures which seemed to threaten their privileges and interests.

Yet after all due allowance has been made for these failures of foresight, and they were great, the judgment expressed by John L. Stephens, United States diplomat, just after Morazán was overthrown by revolution and exiled, remains a fair one. The Central Americans, wrote Stephens,[1] "have cast from their shores the best man of Central America."

[1] Stephens, John L. *Incidents of Travel in Central America*. New York. 1841.

Ironically enough, Francisco Morazán was born in Honduras, one of the countries which has since paid most dearly in petty tyranny the price of the failure of Central American liberalism and unity. He was born in Tegucigalpa, the present capital of that state, in 1792, the year of the first French Republic. His father, Eusebio Morazán, was a French creole from the West Indies, who had settled in Honduras. His mother, Guadalupe Quesada, was a Tegucigalpan. In the private schools of his native city, according to his biographers, young Francisco absorbed the liberal ideas of the French revolutionary philosophy and liberal reform. The only other fact which seems to stand out in his early education was a marked liking for geometry and drawing.

Morazán was a young man of twenty-nine when the independence of Central America, proclaimed immediately following that of Mexico in 1821, gave him his chance. In 1824, the year following the establishment of the Central American Federation, he became secretary general of Honduras, and shortly thereafter its president.

The ill-fated Republic or Federation of Central America was almost immediately precipitated into a confused internal struggle. The principal line of the conflict lay in jealousy by the other states, especially El Salvador, of the preponderant role Guatemala expected to assume in the federation. A second was the conflict between Guatemala and El Salvador growing out of the separation of the church in El Salvador under Bishop Delgado from that of Guatemala. The church had been subordinated to the Salvadoran state, and the latter had inaugurated a more liberal program of reform than the church authorities wished to tolerate. Opposition especially in Guatemala, of creole landowners and churchmen, to the liberalism of many of the leaders of the new federation, was a third line of conflict. These same conservative groups had opposed early tendencies toward Central American independence and had favored the union with Iturbide's Mexico because it promised greater stability and security.

In 1825 an unfortunate disagreement between José Arce and José del Valle, over the first presidential election also helped give the new federation a bad start. Arce, elected president, identified himself with the moderates in opposition to the *exaltados* or liberals. It was the liberal anti-clerical government of the state of Guatemala first, and later of El Salvador and Honduras, which opposed him. The trouble was not so much his lack of liberal sympathies as his loss of the support of his uncle, Delgado, and of the Salvadorans. Whatever the reason, he failed completely to dominate the confused political situation which soon developed. It was a weakness which might have been expected to give the liberal party its desired opportunity. Its effect, however, was rather to bring reactionary forces to the fore in Guatemala.

Morazán entered the situation in 1829 as leader of the military forces of Honduras and El Salvador in the overthrow of the now openly conservative regime. He proceeded at once to a program of liberal reform. Usury laws were abolished; the Archbishop of Guatemala was exiled; monastic orders were suppressed and orders of nuns partially so, and the property of both was confiscated; religious toleration and freedom of speech were established. Honduras established the single tax, abolished the tithe, made the children of priests legitimate heirs of their fathers, and gave priests the right to marry. Guatemala and other states followed suit in one or more of these measures. Several states adopted the jury system and established civil marriage. A new legal code (Livingstone Code) was adopted. How far this liberal spirit extended was shown, perhaps, by the decree of the Federal Congress in 1832 requiring the wearing of mourning for the death of Jeremy Bentham.

The government of Morazán faced frequent rebellions, even though he was supported much of the time in Guatemala by the great liberal chief of that state, Mariano Gálvez. Indian rebellions were a constant threat. The most famous was that led by Anastasio Aquino in El Salvador. But unrest among the Indians was constant and provided one of the bases upon which demagogic caudillos could rise to power through controlling the Indian masses, and through preying on the fears of the landowners. It was one of these caudillos, Rafael Carrera, who finally overthrew Morazán in 1839, with the support of conservatives whose fears and prejudices had been aroused by Morazán's liberalism. Such leaders took advantage also of dissatisfaction produced by the introduction of the jury system and of popular prejudice against the health officials ("poisoners") who tried to introduce new medicines to combat an epidemic of Asiatic cholera.

Even before Carrera's final military triumph in 1840 the Federation had practically fallen to pieces. Rebellion under his leadership was widespread in Guatemala and Costa Rica, while Honduras and Nicuragua had seceded. The Federal Congress had dissolved, summoning a new Federal Constitutional Convention, which never met.

All the liberal reforms were abolished under Carrera's dictatorship which lasted until 1865. In 1842 Morazán returned to Costa Rica from his exile in Peru to attempt to overthrow the Costa Rican dictator Carrillo. But political pessimism and apathy were so widespread that Morazán was unable to arouse the farmers of Costa Rica as he had hoped in a campaign to restore the union. Rebellion broke out, Morazán was handed over to his enemies and shot on September 11, 1842.

Bancroft, Hubert Howe. History of Central America. San Francisco, Bancroft Co. 1882-1887. 3v. v3:p96-144, 216-22.

Montúfar, Manuel. Memorias para la historia de la revolución de Centro-
América, por un Guatemalteco. 4th ed. Guatamala, Tipografía Sánchez
& de Guise. 1934. 280p. First published in Jalapa, Mexico, 1832.
Morazán, Miguel. Francisco Morazán. Washington, Pan American Union.
n.d. 8p. (Tr. by Frances Douglas).
La Prensa. (Buenos Aires). Sept. 13, 1942. Morazán, un precursor. Rafael
Heliodoro Valle.

BERNARDO PEREIRA DE VASCONCELLOS (1795-1850)

Chief of His Majesty's Opposition

A valetudinarian, hated by his contemporaries as few Brazilian leaders have been hated, Bernardo Vasconcellos has an undeserved reputation for Machiavellism. Yet he holds a respectable place in the history of liberal government and in the development of the political institutions of the Republic of Brazil. Defender of liberal monarchy, and leader in laying the basis of parliamentary government under Pedro I, he unfortunately became the symbol of Brazilian reactionary conservatism under the regency during the minority of Pedro II. His realistic perception of the basis upon which a stable political system could be built in Brazil, and his sense of the importance of institutions, suggest at once a striking resemblance to the role of Alexander Hamilton in the United States and to that of Alberdi in Argentina. Yet his record of leadership in Brazilian politics and the amazing number of statutes basic to the juridical system of his country which he fathered, mark him as distinct from either.

He may not be Brazil's greatest statesman, but he is typical of the kind of conservative political leadership which stemmed the tide of separatism in nineteenth century Brazil, and prevented disintegration and chaos. Something in the peculiar turn of events in mid-nineteenth century Brazil, gave Vasconcellos his unique position. Perhaps it was simply that Brazilian independence had not been purchased at the price of a long and costly war of independence as in the other Americas. Something, certainly, in the combination of circumstances in Brazil made it possible for this conservative to carry through a more remarkable constructive parliamentary program than most of his more liberal contemporaries.

Vasconcellos was born in Villa Rica, Minas Geraes, August 27, 1795. He came from a distinguished Portuguese Brazilian family of jurists. Dr. Diogo Pereira Ribeiro Vasconcellos, his father, held numerous offices in Minas Geraes, and was a criminal judge in Rio de Janeiro. His mother, Maria de Carmo Barradas, was the daughter of the Portuguese jurist, João de Sousa Barradas. Her brothers held high positions in Portugal; one of them was a councilor of state.

In 1807, at the age of twelve, Bernardo was sent to Portugal for his education. But the Napoleonic wars and the navy of Great Britain determined otherwise. Captured by the British and turned back to Brazil, Bernardo had no alternative but to complete his preparatory studies there. Six years later, when he set out a second time, the British were in control of Portugal, and his trip was successfully completed. The University of Coimbra in which he enrolled was the center of learning for the Portuguese speaking world. Here Bernardo made an excellent record as a student of law.

Returning to Brazil in 1820 he found that the recent death of his father left him the head of his family. He applied for a magistrate's position and had just assumed his first post, in Guaratinguetá, when Pedro's Grito de Ipiranga made Brazil an independent monarchy in 1822. Vasconcellos was convalescing from a serious illness which had interrupted his official duties shortly after he assumed his position. Nor did he take part in the abortive constitutional convention of 1823.

He was elected in 1824, however, to the Legislative Assembly under the liberal constitution proclaimed by Pedro. During the long delay before the first meeting of the Assembly in 1826, he began (1825) his first association with a journal, O Universal, which was to be the instrument for expressing his political views. It was the first of a series with which his name was connected as editor or contributor: O Sete de Abril, Cabôclo, O Brasileiro, and the Sentinella da Monarchia. His active political career began in the Council for Government of Minas Geraes, the first of the state governments to be organized. In the Council, Vasconcellos took the lead in denouncing the concessions granted by the Crown to two companies: The Diamond Company, and The Society of Agriculture, Commerce, Mining and Navigation of the Rio Dulce, both backed by British capital. It was largely his daring stand which caused the concessions to be defeated.

Opposition to the foreign concessions made Vasconcellos a man of note in the first meeting of the Assembly, even though surrounded by many older leaders from the movement for independence and the Constituent Assembly. Nor was it long until his fearless speech and constructive leadership in the struggle of the Assembly against the Crown made him both feared and respected.

Vasconcellos was a liberal according to many of the standards of his day. He believed in the rights of man and in constitutional, representative government. Defending freedom of speech, freedom of conscience and freedom of the press, he even went so far as to defend the right to attack the form of government. But he was convinced that monarchy was essential to preserve the unity of Brazil, a conviction which grew stronger as the years brought increasing disorder and evidence of separatism. Taking the British constitution as his model, he argued that the way to progress lay in a sound judicial system, in economic and social institutions resting upon a sound legal basis, in reform of the legal system, and in strengthening the prerogatives of the legislative branch in the direction of responsible cabinet and parliamentary government.

In the first session he presented a law requiring ministers to report the state of their departments. He led the Assembly in an investigation of scandals connected with recruiting the army for the war over the possession of Uruguay. In 1827 he introduced his projected reform of the criminal code, based on the social ideas of Jeremy Bentham. The new liberal code finally adopted in 1830 was based largely on his project. The first really national code in Latin America, it has had the greatest influence throughout the continent.

In 1829 as spokesman for the Committee on Finance, he led the Chamber in formulating its first general appropriation bill. Pedro I, following his break with the Andradas, was showing an increasing tendency to despotism. It was this threat of despotism, together with the influence of the Portuguese aristocracy and Pedro's involvement in Portuguese politics, which provided the basis around which the opposition organized, with Vasconcellos as its chief spokesman. Evidence of this leadership appeared clearly when he was appointed to draft his famous reply to the speech from the throne in 1828. It was even more evident in his defense of this reply before the Chamber. After the revolutionary disorders of 1828 he was offered a ministry, but refused. Partly, he said, because he felt he could not dominate the political current and did not want to betray his friends, partly because he wished to retain his leadership in the Chamber.

As in 1822, so in 1831, Vasconcellos appears not to have taken an active part in the Revolution of April 7 which brought the abdication of Pedro in favor of his son. Vasconcellos, the defender of orderly change, disliked revolution. However, once the revolution was over and order restored, he joined forces with Evaristo, editor of *Aurora Flumnense*, and Feijó, who later became regent, in bringing about a reform of institutions. He was named Minister of Justice in 1831. Later, as Secretary of the Treasury (*Fazenda*), he consolidated the government credit and reformed the currency. As Vice President of the Province of Minas Geraes he boldly opposed an uprising in 1833 aimed at the restoration of Pedro I.

The culmination of his reform measures, in many respects the climax of his career, was the *Acto Addicional* of 1834. Favoring decentralization, as he favored monarchy, as a means of controlling the separatism which showed itself in frequent outbursts in Rio Grande do Sul, Pernambuco and elsewhere, he opposed the right of provinces to organize themselves as sovereign states. During the debate in the chamber on the proposals for constitutional change, he pointed out the differences between Brazil and the United States which made federalism impractical in the former, practical in the latter. In the *Acto Addicional* he went no further than partial, practical measures of reform. The *Acto* provided elected provincial assemblies, but not elective provincial executives. At the same time he effectively increased the power of the central government by reducing the number of regents (during the minority of Pedro II) from three to one.

As republicanism grew Vasconcellos became increasingly conservative. The growth of republicanism was dangerous, he thought, since it might mean the break up of Brazil as a nation. This must have been what lay behind his bitter opposition to the continuation of José Bonifacio Andrada as tutor of the young monarch, an opposition which involved him in a bitter struggle with this greatest of the Andradas. But he turned against Feijó also, when the latter, as regent, tried to rule as well as reign. Against his one time collaborator he became once more chief of the opposition, and had no small share in eventually forcing the regent's resignation in 1837. After 1836 he cultivated more and more the political support of large landowners and slave owners, in opposition to republican tendencies. The strength of this group in Brazilian politics is shown in Brazil's persistent refusal to abolish slavery. Vasconcellos saw the same danger in abolition of slavery as in the growing strength of republicanism. This realization, plus his unusual powers of political debate, made him the first effective leader of Brazilian conservative forces.

As minister again in 1837 he reformed the National Guard, granted concessions for steamship navigation between Rio and Pará, and introduced the law establishing the College of Pedro II, the first liberal and literary secondary school of high grade in Brazil. He also established an agricultural school and a botanical garden.

From 1838, when he entered the Senate while still a Minister of State, until his death in 1850, his role was that of leader of a conservative front. When he left the ministry rather than be overthrown over a difference with the regent, the other ministers followed his example. It is interesting to note that in this case he acted contrary to the British principle of ministerial responsibility for which he had fought so hard ten years before. For a brief seven hours he returned to the government as minister in 1840. This brief ministry was a disastrous one, revolving around the conservatives' attempt to thwart the manouevres of the liberals to establish the majority of Young Pedro. Pedro's emphatic *quero já* (I wish it at once), settled the question and brought Vasconcellos' downfall.

Frequently ill, and constantly in pain, he was now often unable to attend to business for days at a time. In the Senate he frequently spoke sitting. Yet in the Senate he was as active as he had previously been in the Chamber. The key to his success as leader of the forces of conservatism lay principally in his realization that all parties were dissatisfied with the strife which had been almost continuous since the days of Pedro I, and wanted peace and order more than anything else. Yet his conservatism did not preclude all interest in reform. He took an important part in formulating a new commercial code and a new criminal code for the nation, and secured adoption of a new law regulating paper currency in 1846. He was also author of a law reforming judicial process, which abolished elective justices of the peace, and he collaborated in another act to revive and reform the Council of State, which had been suppressed by his own *Acto Addicional* of 1834.

Although for personal reasons he was not included in the ministry, the conservative government of 1841 was based on his ideas and was a realization of his political policies. His last political success was the overthrow of the liberal ministry of Alves Branco in 1848. Two years later he died, victim of an epidemic of yellow fever.

This was the famous Deputy Vasconcellos who so intrigued the imagination of the English clergyman Walsh during the days of the regency, that he called him the Franklin or Mirabeau of Brazil. Many an important liberal leader in Latin American democracy must show a much less impressive list of liberal reforms accomplished than this avowed leader of conservatism. He was one of a group of far-seeing Brazilians whose actions prevented the disintegration of their country by the centrifugal forces of separatism. But it was as chief of his majesty's opposition that Vasconcellos played his greatest role and instructed the Brazilian nation in the operation of liberal monarchy.

Calogeras, João Pandiá. A history of Brazil. Chapel Hill, University of North Carolina Press. 1939. 374p. (Ed. and tr. by Percy Alvin Martin).

Tarquinio de Sousa, Octavio. Bernardo Pereira de Vasconcellos e seu tempo. Rio de Janeiro, José Olympio. 1937. 300p.

Benito Pablo Juárez (1806-1872)

Meritorious American

That an Indian could become president of Mexico is enough in itself to indicate how widely Latin American political and social concepts differ from those of Anglo-America. Yet, strangely, this Zapotec Indian, Benito Juárez, stands for little that is racial, in anything like the sense which that term has, for example, in modern Mexican history. Chiefly, he represents nineteenth century liberalism, standing for the freedoms of man; freedom of mind, of religion, and of land.

Conscious Indianism had little place in Latin American social and political development before the twentieth century, and the career of Juárez would have been little different if he had been a descendant of one of the old Spanish families, or a mestizo, rather than an Indian from the mountains of Oaxaca. That a poor Indian boy could make his way to the presidency meant much to the down-trodden Indian masses, of course. And, too, his career illustrates well the socially upsetting process of racial assimilation which lay behind the social and political unrest of his country. Still, Juárez is chiefly significant, not as an Indian, but as a leading protagonist in Mexico's heart-rending struggle to achieve a liberal social order and political constitution.

Benito Pablo Juárez was born of Zapotec parents in the little Indian village of San Pablo de Guelatao, in the state of Oaxaca, March 21, 1806. Orphaned at an early age, he was adopted by an uncle with sufficient means to send him to the city of Oaxaca, where he completed his training for the legal profession. Achievement of Mexican independence in 1821 found Juárez at an impressionable age, just beginning his university career. Revolutionary feeling ran high in Oaxaca, center of the old Zapotec civilization, and one of the most stubbornly Indian regions of Mexico. Oaxaca had seen some of the bloodiest incidents of the fighting of the previous decade, when revolutionary forces, led by the curates Hidalgo and Morelos, had encountered a reactionary political, social and religious hierachy. Nothing could have been more natural than for the young Indian law student, deeply moved by the wrongs of his fellow Indians, to throw himself heart and soul into the cause of the Liberals who were now seeking, against the opposition of conservative church leaders and landholders, to bring about a reform of the Church and the land system.

From 1833 to 1847 the Liberals were frequently in control in Mexico, trying with little success to carry out their program of reform. Juárez was elected deputy to the Federal Congress and governor of his state. He turned Oaxaca into the most prosperous and orderly province in Mexico, and gathered around him a group of liberal and idealistic leaders who were to dominate Mexican life for years to come. When the Conservatives returned to power in the midst of the war with the United States, Juárez withdrew from public life. He was persecuted, imprisoned, and finally driven into exile by Santa Ana. Then in 1855 he returned to office with the Liberal revolutionary movement led by Álvarez, became a minister in the Álvarez cabinet, and helped formulate the program of liberal reform which occupied the center of political controversy during the following years.

In 1857 he became president. During the next twenty-five years, until his death in 1872, Mexican history centered around the life of the little Oaxaca Indian. Captured once by the Zuloaga Conservatives and placed before a firing squad, tradition has it that he was miraculously saved by the brave outcry of Mexico's great poet, Guillermo Prieto, "Soldiers, shoot over his head! Brave men do not murder!" Whatever the truth of the tradition, it represents well the extent to which Mexican life had come to revolve around him. Finally, in 1861, he was able to establish himself again in Mexico City, only to face the intervention of France, Spain and Great Britain in protest against his suspension of payments of the foreign debt.

Now followed the desperate struggle against Maximilian and the French, which ended only when the demands of the United States, combined with Maximilian's alienation of his conservative Mexican support and the growing seriousness of France's international situation, caused Napoleon III to withdraw the French troops. Juárez captured and executed Maximilian in 1867. Only then was he free to carry out the liberal program of reforms incorporated in his Constitution of 1857 and in the laws of reform of the previous decade; laws nationalizing church property, separating church and state, establishing religious toleration, secularizing education and marriage, and in various ways altering the land system.

To Juárez it seemed impossible for Mexico to achieve democracy in the presence of a rich, powerful, and reactionary state church which owned a large part of the land, dominated banking, and controlled the thinking of a large part of the population. But it was not anti-religious feeling so much as a liberal economic and social philosophy which prompted his program. Mexico, under his leadership, became the first nation of Latin America to separate church and state completely. In spite of the bitter conflict produced by his church reforms, and in the face of seemingly insurmountable complications in his relations with the United States, France and other powers, he gave Mexico her greatest liberal regime prior to the Revolution of 1910. Although his program was prostituted soon after his death by the dictatorship of his young Oaxacan lieutenant, Porfirio Díaz, still, the Juárez reforms were the solid basis on which Díaz built his more ephemeral success.

Today, as one stands on the hill outside Oaxaca, before Cencetti's heroic bronze statue of the Oaxacan liberal, and reads the single word REFORM in the book he holds in his hand, one realizes with what justice Benito Juárez received from his government the title of Meritorious American.

Probably nowhere else on the American continent has one man tried so much against such great obstacles as Juárez tried in Mexico in the name of the principle of social and economic liberalism. It was Victor Hugo who singled him out as the second great liberal spirit of America. "America has produced two great men, Abraham Lincoln and thee," wrote the great Frenchman to the great Mexican. Whatever one may think of the relative merits of the two men, the judgment of history seems to be that the task of Juárez was the harder.

Bancroft, Hubert Howe. Chronicles of the builders of the commonwealth. San Francisco, History Co. 1891-1892. v.1:162-224.

Bulnes, Francisco. Juárez y las revoluciones de Ayutla y de reforma. Mexico. 1905. 651p.

Burke, Ulrick Ralph. A life of Benito Juárez, constitutional president of Mexico. London and Sydney, Remington & Co. 1894. 384p.

Nava de Ruisánchez, Julia. Benito Juárez. (Pan American Patriots series). Washington, Pan American Union. n.d. 8p.

Sierra, Justo. Juárez; su obra y su tiempo. Mexico, J. Ballesca y compania, sucesores. 1905-1908. 500p.

Werfel, Franz W. Juárez and Maximilian. (Theatre Guild version) New York, Simon and Schuster. 1926. n.p. (Tr. by Ruth Langner).

José Julián Martí (1853-1895)

Poet Rebel

Among the many poets of Latin America José Martí is uniquely representative of the great struggle for democracy. In pain and sorrow he lived his life as a poem. He led the Cubans to complete the great American epic of freedom by the independence of Cuba. His martyrdom gave that epic its tragic fulfillment.

Martí lived in an age of disillusionment. By the time of his birth in 1853 the old revolutionary idealism was largely gone. The generation of liberators had too often seen their fond dreams of free independent republics in America degenerate into the chaos and brutality of caudillo rule. Even those republics which had achieved political stability and prosperity had all too frequently reverted to political and cultural colonialism under the dominance of a timid, conservative oligarchy of landowners, usually relying on military rulers.

Yet the cause of freedom and democracy was not dead, as Martí showed. Discredited and discouraged by the overwhelming tenacity of the colonial economic system, the lack of racial and social homogeneity, and the absence of an invigorating commercial interest and class, it was dormant but still alive in the minds and hearts of a saddened and wiser generation. It still lived in stubborn movements of liberal protest against military dictators, and in the Cuban independence movement. Martí, poet-philosopher, realized that romantic idealism could not be revived, but that a belief in democracy could be. He preached a revolution based on a passion for decorum and the dignity of man, joined to an appeal to all Latin Americans to seek their destiny in their own historical origins, not in foreign ideas and institutions—a union of Bolívar and Spencer, he called it.

José Martí came to maturity during the desperate Ten Years War for Cuban independence which began in 1868. At the age of thirteen he entered the Colegio of San Pablo, where he studied under Rafael María de Mendive, revolutionary poet and journalist. Mendive was imprisoned by the Spanish authorities that same year (1866) for his revolutionary sympathies. A visit to his imprisoned teacher made a deep impression on José's young mind. From that date till his death twenty-nine years later, his romantic spirit never faltered in passionate devotion to the revolutionary cause. While he was studying in the Instituto de Segunda Enseñanza under Cristóbal Madán, he published his first revolutionary poem, "Abdala," in *La Patria Libre* edited by Mendive and Madán. A few months later he was arrested because of a letter he and Valdés Domínguez had written to a former student of Mendive, who was then in the Spanish service, accusing him of apostasy and urging him to return to the Cuban cause. Rashly and defiantly the sixteen-year-old Martí claimed sole authorship of the letter and made such a fiery plea for Cuban independence at his trial that the Spanish officer in charge demanded the penalty of death for him. Instead, the military court sentenced both boys to six years imprisonment at hard labor.

Sickness and death were frequent among the prisoners working in the limestone quarry of San Lazaro, and Martí's frail strength soon broke. The iron grill on his ankle wounded him severely, producing a cancerous growth which later required several surgical operations for its cure. The experience left a permanent mark on his health. At the end of two months, sick physically and at heart, his eyes burned by the limestone dust, and his spirit revolted by indiscriminate association with hardened criminals, he was at last released. He had inspired such sympathy in the owner of the quarries, Sardá, that the latter secured his transfer to the Isle of Pines, where he remained under Sardá's personal charge until permitted to go to Spain in 1870 to continue his studies.

He arrived in a Spain charged with the atmosphere of civil war. Spain was undergoing a kaleidoscopic series of governments from the overthrow of Queen Isabella in 1868, through the Hohenzollern candidacy, the unstable rule of Amadeo I, the short-lived republic of 1873-74, to the restoration of monarchy under Alfonso XII. Martí naturally became as much revolutionary agitator as student. Shortly after his arrival he published a scathing denunciation of Spanish treatment of political prisoners in Cuba, "The Political Prison in Cuba," full of the emotion of his own experience. His poetic ode to the student demonstrators shot on the streets of Havana on November 27, 1871, was electric in its effect upon public opinion in Spain. In Zaragosa during the historic siege, he stirred up the republican sympathies of the city with his fiery oratory. After the establishment of the Republic he pleaded the Cuban cause personally with the government and in a pamphlet, "The Spanish Republic Confronting the Cuban Revolution."

The twenty-one-year-old man who limped off the boat in Vera Cruz, Mexico, in 1874, his education completed, was already a poet-revolutionist of international reputation. In Mexico he edited a journal and devoted himself to writing. He was impressed especially by the tendency to copy things European which he saw around him, and began to urge the development of an American education, literature and thought, an American way of life, and American economic and political institutions. In 1877 he was in Guatemala, lecturing in the Normal School and publishing the *Revista Guatemalteca*. He went to Cuba again after the Ten Years War was over, but was soon imprisoned and again deported in 1878 for his connection with a rebellion in Oriente. Escaping from prison in Spain he made his way to Paris, to New York, and finally to Caracas, Venezuela. "I will arouse the world," he said in Caracas. "The poem of 1810 is incomplete, and I wish to write the last strophe."

The twenty-eight-year-old Martí who sailed for New York a few months later to devote the next fourteen years to plotting Cuban independence was the recognized intellectual and moral leader of the Cuban cause. During the Ten Years War the revolutionists had proclaimed the abolition of slavery. Martí now proclaimed that in Cuba there was but one race, the Cuban, and through his passionate appeals for the union of Negro and white in the common cause of Cuban independence made himself the almost deified leader of the Cuban Negroes.

It was a terrible blow when United States authorities stopped the departure of two vessels equipped with much labor and expense for a filibustering expedition to initiate the new revolution. But Martí and his companions, undaunted, made their way to Cuba and began hostilities on February 24, 1895. On May 19, at Dos Ríos, disobeying General Máximo Gómez, he joined the first charge of the rebels and was killed. Cuban independence completed the great American epic, and Martí, as he had said he would, wrote the last Byronic strophe, but with a martyr's blood.

Although Martí thus marks the end of an historical epoch, he also epitomizes the progress of Latin America from the ideas of the French Revolution toward new social concepts responding to the new forces of nineteenth century industrialism, economic nationalism and imperialism. He decried the easy acceptance of the political incapacity of Latin Americans to which the prevalent Positivist ideas contributed. Ideas to him were weapons and his clear call for a spiritual revolution as the basis of the political, social and economic redemption sounded the keynote of the twentieth century in Latin American social thought. Martí was the proto-type, as he became the idol, of the next generation of Latin American youth.

Crawford, W. Rex. A century of Latin-American thought. Cambridge, Mass., Harvard University Press. 1944. p228-36.

Ghiraldo, Alberto. Libertadores de América. Santiago de Chile, Ercilla. 1935. p175-202.

Lizaso, Félix. Martí y la Utopía de América. La Habana, García y Cía. 1942. 7-46p.

Mañach, Jorge. Martí, el apóstol, Madrid, 1933. Selection in English translation in Arciniegas, Germán, ed. The green continent. New York, Knopf. 1944. p318-37.

Martí, José. Pensamiento de América, prólogo y ·selección de Mauricio Magdaleno. Mexico, Ediciones Botas. 1942. 231p.

Martínez Bello, Antonio. Ideas sociales y económicas de José Martí. La Habana, La Verónica. 1940. 219p.

Mijares, Augusto. Hombres e ideas en América. Caracas, Escuela Técnica Industrial. 1940. p77-112.

MANUEL GONZÁLEZ PRADA (1848-1918)

Maestro of Peruvian Youth

The failures of nineteenth century Latin America to achieve a stable, social basis for the political organization of freedom was devastating in its effect on the forces of liberalism. Caudillism and the military dictatorships which sprang up in the moral vacuum created by these failures brought exile, oppression and destruction to such liberal leaders as remained. Yet, somehow, a few men retained confidence in the ability of their countrymen to act politically, kept the spirit of liberty alive, and by their examples inspired the Mariáteguis and Haya de la Torres of the present generation. Such was Manuel González Prada of Peru.

For years González Prada was the Peruvian conscience. His pen was constantly active in the denunciation of his country's social and political errors and vices, the anarchy and political corruption which he pointed out as the real cause of military defeat which Peru received at the hands of Chile in 1879. Of all Peruvians he came nearest to being the counterpart of Argentina's Sarmiento, Alberdi, Mitre and Avellaneda.

He was born in Lima in 1848, the third son of Francisco González de Prada and Josefa Alvárez de Ulloa. His mother came from an old and wealthy family of Arequipa, his father from one of the oldest and most distinguished noble families of Spain and Peru. His ancestors included officials of importance in the courts of Charles V, Philip II, and Philip III, and under the viceroyalty. On his mother's side was the famous Antonio Ulloa, of the *Noticias Secretas*, the first comprehensive picture presented to the Spanish crown of the causes of the unrest seething in America in the eighteenth century. His grandfather, Josef González de Prada y Falcón came to America in 1784, just as the rebellion of Tupac Amaru was being suppressed, and married Doña Nicolosa de Marrón y Lombera, daughter of one of the greatest Spanish generals of the day in America. Don Josef won a position of high confidence in the last days of the viceroyalty, and his defeat of the rebels at the bridge of Ambo would have brought him a Spanish noble title as the Count of Ambo, except for the disorders of the times.

Francisco, son of Don Josef and father of Manuel, was born in 1815, in the days of the Indian revolt of Pumacahua. After studying law in the University of Chuquisaca, he moved to Arequipa, and later to Lima in Peru. Don Francisco represented the most conservative influences of conservative Peru. He was more "Godo" (Conservative Party) than the

"Godos," and had a great horror of liberalism in all forms. Doña Josefa was fanatically religious. The home of the González de Pradas, on the Calle de Piedra in Lima, was a home of wealth, constantly filled with relatives and guests, but like a convent in atmosphere. Under the montonero President Castilla there was little place in political life for a representative of an "old family," but under his successor, Echenique, "old families" got their chance again. Don Francisco was appointed minister to Bolivia.

His political career was short. Another revolution sent the González de Pradas into political exile in Chile. Here young Manuel attended the Colegio Inglés, learning both English and German. When his family returned to Lima, he entered the Seminary of Santo Toribio. Then, in 1861, a thirteen-year-old boy with large, calm blue eyes and rosy cheeks, he entered the Colegio de San Carlos. The Colegio de San Carlos was noted for its free discussion of political, social and literary topics, and Don Francisco must have hesitated long before sending his son there. Needless to say, the religious Doña Josefa, was disturbed. For Manuel this newly found freedom was the beginning of a new life.

His father's death found him studying law in the University according to his mother's wish, although against his own. He gave up law at the end of the year. The next years were spent managing a family estate in the Mala valley, near Cañete. His work left him long hours of leisure. Pursuing an interest in chemistry developed at the Colegio de San Carlos, he began research to discover a new industrial product from yucca, much to the mystification of the natives. He also began to write poems, some of which appeared in *El Correo de Peru.*

The first clear statement of his opposition to the prevailing political corruption of the day was his prologue to a book of Aureliane Villarán's poems, published in 1879. The War of the Pacific intervened, but after serving in the Peruvian army during the Siege of Callao, he took up the fight in earnest against the militarists who dominated politics after Peru's disastrous defeat. A free thinker from his student days, and an admirer of the free-thinking librarian of the *Biblioteca Nacional*, Vigil, he naturally directed much of his criticism, also, against clericalism and the superstition upon which it throve.

It was in the period following the war that González Prada rose to his greatest importance. Peru in these years was passing through the most serious crisis of her national life. Twice defeated in war with her aggressive neighbor to the south, the once rich and great viceroyalty was sinking to the level of the lesser states among the progeny of the Spanish motherland. The social forces which still ruled Peruvian society, in spite of the movement for independence and the liberalism of the mid-century, were colonial, even feudal. It was hard for the old families who had always dominated Peruvian politics to see that national regeneration and a generous program of social and political action were essential to the development of nationality.

On September 11, 1887, Manuel married a French girl, Adrienne Verneuil, whom he had first met ten years before as a young girl at his parents' home. The marriage was an exceptionally happy one. Adrienne shared his literary tastes and came also to share his political views. The death in infancy of her first two children brought her even to share his religious free thinking.

On July 29, 1888, at a festival in the Teatro Politeama, González Prada delivered the address which made him thereafter the idol, the "maestro" of Peruvian student youth. "Old men to their graves, young men to their tasks," was his stirring cry against the old forces of traditionalism and corruption. Later, at the Teatro Olympo, his outburst against academicism, colonialism and traditionalism brought him into opposition to the other great Peruvian writer of his day, the traditionalist Ricardo Palma.

So far his activity had centered in the *Círculo Literario*, a group of liberal writers. Now (1891) he assisted in forming the *Unión Nacional*, a political party, to agitate for these progressive ideas. Its program included restoration of Indian lands, modification of the Indian tribute, direct elections, improvement of the conditions of workers, obligatory representation of minorities in Congress, and parliamentary or congressional responsibility.

Political activity, and especially the agitation centering around the assassination of the Ecuadorean dictator, García Moreno, brought a self-imposed exile to Paris for seven years, 1891-1898. For Adrienne this was a period of homecoming to which she would always look back with nostalgia. Here her son Alfredo was born. Manuel too, discovered a successor to his beloved Vigil, in Renan. He attended meetings of free thinkers and came under the influence of socialism. Returning to Lima in 1898, he reassumed leadership of the party, but soon left it because he felt the party was too willing to compromise with the petty politics of the day. His own activity took a more uncompromising tone, as in his famous speech to the Bakers' Union in 1905. In this speech he set the keynote for a new age of Peruvian political leadership in a plea for the union of intellectuals with workers.

When *La Nación* of Buenos Aires invited him to contribute to their columns, it was an indication that his writing was at last winning continental recognition. His first article dealt with the social function of poetry. It was reprinted in *El Comercio* of Cuzco and created a literary storm in Peru comparable to the political effect of his 1888 speech.

When Ricardo Palma resigned as librarian of the *Biblioteca Nacional*, because of a quarrel over library appointments, González Prada took his place. Even the old traditionalist agreed that there was no other literary personage so deserving of the place as González Prada. Yet the latter held the post only two years, 1912-1914, under the most bitter criticism, until he was removed by the Benavides *coup d'etat*. Two years later, fortunately, another change in politics returned him to the library.

It was here that young Víctor Raúl Haya de la Torre, destined soon to become the leader of Peruvian student youth, found him. To the younger man, discouraged in his efforts toward university reform, the warmth of the old leader's generous spirit was just what was needed, if we are to believe Haya's account, to make him decide to give his own life to the cause of reform. About a year later (1918) the voice of the maestro of Peruvian youth was stilled in death.

In his *Horas de lucha* and his *Páginas libres*, González Prada was the spirit of national redemption and regeneration. The twentieth century, indeed, finds it hard to understand the hate which he preached against Chile. But his indictment of official corruption and inefficiency, of the lack of popular education, of the stupidity and shortsightedness of the landowning aristocracy, of the stagnation of industry and commerce, and of the economic disparities between the classes of society, elevates him to the level of the best of the brave and humane leaders of the cause of Latin American democracy. Like the great Uruguayan idealist Rodó, he saw his greatest duty in filling the enormous spiritual vacuum of his national literature. To this end he developed an idealism which was both humane and contagious in its influence on Peruvian youth, and was conceived in the social needs of his day.

Much has been written in praise of Peru's great liberal spirit, but certainly no finer epitaph than the simple verse of the Peruvian poet, José Lora y Lora, who died tragically under the wheels of the Paris Metro:

> Here is the plan of a project of mine:
> The plinth, a verse of Ruben Darío;
> The statue, a phrase of González Prada.

Blanco-Fombona, Rufino. Grandes escritores de América (Siglo XIX). Madrid, Renacimiento. 1917. p267-325.

Crawford, W. Rex. A century of Latin-American thought. Cambridge, Mass., Harvard University Press. 1944. p173-82.

Melián Lafinur, Álvaro. Figuras Americanas. Paris, Casa Editorial Franco-Ibero-Americana. 1926. p141-9.

American Mercury. 6:330-3. November 1925. A Peruvian iconoclast. Isaac Goldberg.

Hispania. 6:299-308. November 1923. Peruvian literature. George W. Umpherey.

Hispanic American Historical Review. 23:424-40. August 1943. Intellectual origins of Aprismo. Robert Edwards McNicoll.

Panorama. 22:15-22. June 1943. ˉManuel González Prada. Bibliography. (Published by the Pan American Union).

Revista Hispanica Moderna. 4:51. October 1938. González Prada, vida y obra—bibliografía—antología. (Published by the Instituto de las Españas en los Estados Unidos, New York).

Part III

Latin American Makers of Democracy Today

THE RESURGENCE OF POLITICAL LEADERSHIP

By the end of the nineteenth century Latin America was saddened and disillusioned. Political leadership of the heroic caliber of Sarmiento, Mitre, and Juárez had disappeared from the scene. Balmaceda in Chile and José Martí in Cuba were the last of the great nineteenth century liberals. The former took his own life in desperation, overwhelmed by the forces of conservativism and localism in the landowning oligarchy which dominated the Chilean congress. Martí, on the other hand, through his magnificent poetry, and by his martyr's death in the war for Cuban independence, became a connecting link between the old and the new. In the movement for Cuban independence he fired a new generation of Latin American youth with a belief in their own destiny.

Latin Americans had generally become willing to accept the limitations and shortcomings of their political and social life as inevitable and incapable of any remedy except such as time would bring. The owners of land, often with the cooperation of high officials of the church who were drawn from the same landowning families, had joined forces with the military and political system in which the mestizo class was finding its political expression in many of the states. The union had brought in most cases a kind of political stability. It was a precarious political balance, to be sure, which scarcely hid from sight the deep-lying social problems of race, land, education and labor which remained unsolved. Yet to a chastened generation, even of liberal leadership, it could well seem preferable to the chaos and anarchy of the early part of the century. Even the revolutions which still came all too frequently in some countries represented chiefly some shift of the political classes around the military system, and left untouched the basic sources of political power.

García Calderón evolved the theory which justified it all. Latin Americans, because of their political inexperience, ignorance, poverty and illiteracy and because of their mixed racial and cultural backgrounds could not establish an orderly, peaceful and progressive society by means of democratic institutions and methods of government, at least not at once. They must find their destiny, instead, by turning to the only real and strong element which had appeared in their politics since independence, the caudillo or local strong man, who owed his strength to control of the local military forces, and to his archetype the super-caudillo dictator. All efforts to introduce the masses into the free functioning of the political order had produced only anarchy and bloodshed. Dictatorship alone could maintain order and produce the prosperity which was an essential condition to any other reforms, including education. Revolution-ridden Mexico seemed to be setting the example for her sister republics in the benevolent dictatorship of Porfirio Díaz. But elsewhere, too, a dozen lesser Díazes found acceptance among the substantial citizens of all classes, and were lauded in intellectual and university circles.

Even the brilliant liberal Uruguayan philosopher, José Enrique Rodó, urged Latin American youth to cultivate closer ties with Spain and the Spanish heritage. In his *Ariel*, a book of great influence among the younger generation, he urged a kind of cool Parnassian spiritualism. The great Venezuelan liberal, Rufino Blanco-Fombona, whose *Aladdin's Lamp* was almost if not quite the equal of Rodó's *Ariel* in its influence, represented life as a struggle between good and evil in which evil often won. Ideas of this sort might steel liberal spirits to patient suffering of the evils of society, and did undoubtedly influence the development of many fine liberal spirits. But more young hearts were fired by the martyrdom of the heroic poet, Martí. And elsewhere, in Argentina, Uruguay, Chile, Peru and Mexico, teachers, writers and political leaders commenced to appear in the years just preceding the First World War, renouncing the cynicism, the disillusionment, and the cool objectivism of their elders. Here was a new generation, a resurging optimistic leadership, which was convinced that the social and economic problems of their unhappy countries could be solved by political action. The flame was fed further by Rubén Darío's new poetry and by the theories of Carlos Bunge in his *Nuestra América*.

In Mexico the turbulence of the years following the overthrow of the Díaz dictatorship gave this new leadership a chance to show its influence. Elsewhere it moved more slowly through organizations of students, through the development of labor unions, through music, literature and painting, through political organization and agitation, even through army circles, usually the mainstay of Latin American conservatism.

José Ingenieros, brilliant physician, psychologist and criminologist urged the cultivation of a new spirituality in his *Mediocre Man*, but also, in his writing and by his own example encouraged a new optimism in political leadership. Roque Sáenz Peña, radical president of Argentina (1910-1916), not only led his nation in electoral reform, but into a new policy of internationalism as well, through participation in the ABC bloc and its friendly services in the Niagara Conferences which tried to settle the difficulties in Mexico. He was followed by the first "President of the People" in Argentina, Hipólito Irigoyen.

In Uruguay José Batlle appeared as the leader of a determined group of young reformers which succeeded in transforming that anarchic buffer state into one of the continent's most stable and progressive. The Atheneum in Mexico was a group of young intellectuals, artists and professional men, out of which appeared such prominent figures in Mexico's Revolution as Diego Rivera, José Vasconcelos, Antonio Caso, and Alfonso Reyes. In the fields of art, education, philosophy and literature, respectively, these four men are typically representative of the return of this new confidence in political action. The next Mexican generation produced the brilliant political leadership of Lázaro Cárdenas and Vicente Lombardo Toledano. In Chile Alessandri was able to rally enough support to defeat the strongly entrenched forces of conservatism which had destroyed Balmaceda.

But the most striking manifestation of the new leadership may be seen in the spectacular appearance in most Latin American countries, even in the face of dictatorial opposition, of vigorous, well organized student movements, demanding university reform, identifying themselves with the cause of the downtrodden mãsses, and seeking out the leadership of the incipient labor organizations for cooperation. Out of this movement came two Peruvians whose figures assume continental proportions, the brilliant tubercular young journalist, Mariátegui, and the leader of the APRA (Association for American Revolution), Víctor Raúl Haya de la Torre. Mariátegui and Haya de la Torre conceived a social and political movement on a continental scale, or coextensive at least with Spanish America. In many ways it was the *Nuestra América* of Carlos Bunge. Their method was the union of students with organized workers to awaken the Indian masses and other "under-dog" groups in a radical solution of the basic Latin American problems of land, illiteracy, poverty and race.

But the new generation of leadership is not always consistent, and not always clear in its aims. Madero and Alessandri, for example, were strongly influenced by nineteenth century liberalism, while Mariátegui and Lombardo Toledano, to cite two examples from many, show strong Marxist influences. Many of the new leaders are ardent Yankee haters, although some have also been ardent Pan Americanists. Most have shown traits of nationalism, although some, even those of the most marked nationalistic tendencies, have paid at least verbal respect to a revived interest in Spanish or Hispanic American unity, or to Pan Hispanism. The chief common interest which unites them is confidence in furthering the welfare of the under-dog by political action.

JOSÉ BATLLE Y ORDÓÑEZ (1865-1929)

Uruguayan Reformer President

Only the fact that Uruguay is a small nation of two millions, situated far south of the equator, keeps it from being one of the most talked of nations of the world for its liberal, progressive government. And if José Batlle y Ordóñez had been the reforming chief executive of any one of the states of Europe, or of the United States, he would be known as one of the world's great benefactors. The history of Latin America, certainly, holds no parallel to the breath-taking success with which José Batlle and his followers, by democratic and peaceful means, transformed revolution-ridden, caudillo-ruled Uruguay of the nineteenth century—border Uruguay, which had been for so long the victim of Argentine and Brazilian rival territorial ambitions and of European intervention—into the most progressive, peaceful, and socially conscious nation of South America. For modern Uruguay is uniquely the product of the clear vision, brilliant leadership, and singleness of purpose of José Batlle and his idealistic and enthusiastic young followers.

Born in 1865, Batlle, like most Uruguayan youths of good family, went to Europe for his education. Returning in 1882, he at once entered actively into the politics of the day. He founded a newspaper, *El Día*, devoted to a campaign for democratic reform of his country, and identified himself with the Colorado Party, the party historically committed to the interests of the peasants and to reform, as opposed to the more conservative Blancos. By 1903 he had made himself powerful enough politically to be elected president. Faced with the customary revolt of the Blancos, he offered them a coalition government in the interest of peace. When they refused and took up arms, he defeated them decisively in the battle of Masoller, September 1, 1904. This was the last resort to violent revolution in Uruguayan politics.

Contrary to precedent, he did not try to perpetuate himself in office, but gave way to his successor at the expiration of his four-year term, and left for Europe. The next four years he devoted to study and writing, evolving the most comprehensive and radical program for the solution of the problems of a Latin American country which had yet been seen. Only Bolívar's proposal for a life-term presidency, with an organized fourth, or moral power of government, and the establishment of parliamentary cabinet government in Chile after the Revolution of 1890, are comparable. Political instability in Latin America, he urged, was due to two things: the existence of deep rooted, unsolved, social problems, and the concentration of political power in the hands of the executive, the latter the natural result of the former, as Bolívar had seen. Political stability was a necessary condition to social reform. But the solution, he felt, could not be found either through the secret compulsory ballot which was being urged in Argentina, or through the parliamentary system of Chile, since Latin America was not really prepared for either. Instead, from study of the Swiss constitution, he developed his proposal for a collegiate executive with divided executive power, assuming that the solution might be found in a group of men rather than a single individual taking power and responsibility.

These views, announced in *El Día* shortly after his re-election to the presidency in 1911, startled the nation and prompted one of the most vigorous and brilliant political arguments ever known in Latin America. Subordinating every other political consideration to his proposed constitutional reform, Batlle demanded and secured a constitutional convention which met in the fall of 1917. Yet, when the convention met he and his followers found themselves outnumbered, and only by the most persuasive arguments, and by brilliant compromise, succeeded in changing what looked like a defeat into a victory.

The presidency was not abolished, but was combined with an executive council of nine, with powers of its own. A number of boards and departments were given practical autonomy, so as to remove them from executive control and political influence. The constitutional basis was also laid for minority representation and for the program of social legislation which came to include a comprehensive program of old age and invalid pensions, pensions for school teachers and other public employees, minimum wage laws for rural as well as city workers, laws regulating the labor of women and children, provisions for public health aiming ultimately at free medical treatment for every citizen, and a comprehensive system of public education which soon made education the largest item in the budget aside from service of the national debt. State corporations were established to operate banks, docks, railways, electric utilities, street railways, telegraphs, telephones, the national refrigerating plant, and monopolies such as alcohol and petroleum.

Uruguay seemed too stable and prosperous to be affected by the wave of revolution which swept Latin America in 1930. But in 1933 President Gabriel Terra executed a bloodless *coup d'etat*, which in 1934 brought some constitutional changes. A president and cabinet responsible to congress were substituted for the previous dual executive, and several of the formerly autonomous state corporations were subordinated to the executive. In 1942 President Baldomir was forced to go still further in the direction of strengthening the position of the executive, and weakening the power of the minority party in the Senate.

Again Bolívar's principle of the strong executive seems to have been corroborated. But the Batlle social reforms remain unchanged. In some respects Terra's *coup d'etat*, the new constitution and the more recent changes seem even to have extended the reforms. Thus completely has Uruguay been transformed within a brief quarter of a century by the work of this brilliant maker of democracy, whose lifelong motto was "The easing of human suffering!"

Inman, Samuel Guy. Latin America, its place in world life. Rev. ed. New York, Harcourt, Brace. 1942. p246-51.

Rippy, J. Fred. Historical evolution of Hispanic America. 2nd ed. New York, F. S. Crofts. 1940. p283-6.

Hispanic American Historical Review. 10:413-28. November 1930. The career of José Batlle y Ordóñez. Percy A. Martin.

José Carlos Mariátegui (1895-1930)

Voice of the Disinherited

When, in 1930, the students of Buenos Aires invited the brilliant but invalid Peruvian liberal poet and writer, José Carlos Mariátegui, to come to Argentina to continue his campaign for the redemption of the Indian and landless masses of Latin America, they were not thinking of the historical symbolism of their invitation. Yet, as Waldo Frank wrote at the time, the coming of this warrior of thought from Peru to Argentina, had death not prevented it, would have completed an historical cycle begun a hundred years before with the coming of San Martín and his grenadiers to liberate Peru from Spain. For the sickly, emaciated figure of Mariátegui, with penetrating feverish eyes, was a symbol of all the ills as well as the hopes of Peru. With his high cheek bones, wide-spread ears and acquiline nose, he typified the mixed racial inheritance of Indo-America and represented the new youthful political generation of Latin America which was determined to end once and for all the political and military oligarchies inherited from the movement for independence.

Mariátegui came up from the slums of Lima. Lima is one of America's most beautiful cities, of which the hemisphere may well be proud. But it also, at least until very recent times, has had some very bad tuberculosis-breeding slums. He was born in 1895, a year marked by outbreak of the Cuban Revolution inspired by the poet José Martí, and by the overthrow of the military dictatorship of General Cáceres in Peru. Mariátegui grew up in poverty, undernourished, cared for only by his devoted mother. A childhood accident to his knee, which never healed properly because of mal-nutrition, was to cause him life-long pain, making him an invalid before the age of thirty, and bringing an early death at thirty-five.

At the age of twelve his formal schooling stopped, and he entered a Lima printing shop as copyboy. Running errands through the streets of Lima in constant pain, or occasionally riding the tramways, he continued his self-education by reading chance books and newspapers. By the time he was sixteen he had learned the trade of typesetting, and at eighteen had become one of Peru's most brilliant journalists, supporting himself, as well as his mother and a brother and sister, with his pen.

Mariátegui began to write in an age in which the great literary figures of the older generation were the traditionalist Ricardo Palma and the inspired, fighting liberal prophet, Manuel González Prada. Like them, he inevitably reflected political tendencies in his writing, even in the D'Annunzio-like poetry which he wrote under various pseudonyms. In opposition to the heterodox "futurism" of a group of young writers led by the critic Riva Agüero, Mariátegui and a group of young writers organized the Colónida movement, with tendencies similar to the popular political movement led by Augusto Leguía, the later dictator.

This was during the years 1915-18, and Mariátegui's name was just beginning to receive national attention, particularly because of two incidents. The first was a sensational article he wrote in the newspaper, *El Tiempo*, analyzing and criticizing the experience and qualifications of the officers of the politics-ridden army. A group of officers stung with the sharpness of his lashing attack, invaded the newspaper office and visited their vengeance on the young crippled author with a vicious beating. The second incident was more bizarre, and more scandalous. Mariátegui, with a group of young poets, artists and musicians invited the dancer Norka Ruscaya, then in Lima, to dance for them at night in a cemetery to the music of Chopin's Funeral March. When it became known, the nation was scandalized by this "profaning of ashes" and "sacrilege of tombs," as it was called in a debate in Congress. All the participants, including the dancer, were arrested and threatened with imprisonment until the intervention of some of the leading liberals and men of letters brought their release.

For the support of his pen in the election of 1918, Mariátegui was rewarded by the newly installed Leguía administration with a fellowship for study and travel in Europe. It was the turning point in his career. Studying the political and intellectual leadership of postwar Europe, and its swirling maelstrom of social movements, he began to evolve a theory of political leadership and of social renovation for his own Peru. He was impressed especially with the agrarian aspects of the Russian Revolution, with Lenin as the intellectual leader of a great movement of social change, and with the political genius of Lloyd George.

Returning to Peru, he became involved in the organizations of students, and in the student revolts of the 'twenties against the now reactionary Leguía regime. Living in poverty in the slums of Lima, he became the voice of the disinherited. In the magazine *Amauta*, which he founded in 1926, and in his books, especially his *Seven Essays on Peruvian Reality*, he elaborated a program which was intended to bring social and political freedom to Peru, and to redeem the Indian pariahs from their social ostracism. His "Essay on the Problem of the Land" struck at the heart of the land monopoly, and at the oligarchy of landholders allied with foreign commercial and mining interests which dominated politics. They were responsible, he argued, for the nation's economic backwardness, as well as for dictatorship, militarism, and political disorder. He called for land distribution, and a program of advanced social legislation.

Not since the days of Sarmiento and Alberdi had so clear and comprehensive a program of social reform become the center of a great social and political movement in Latin America. Working under constant persecution of the Leguía administration, and knowing that death from tuberculosis was a matter of months or a few years at the best, Mariátegui refused to be silenced until 1930, when his proposed move to Argentina was prevented by his death. Yet even before death closed his eyes, the Popular Alliance for American Revolution (APRA), based on his program although repudiating his Marxist tendencies, had been organized under the leadership of his friend and collaborator, Raúl Haya de la Torre.

Bazán, Armando. José Carlos Mariátegui. Santiago de Chile, Zig-zag. 1939. 136p.

Carrión, Benjamín. Mapa de América. Madrid, Sociedad General Española de Libraría. 1930. p195-225.

Crawford, W. Rex. A century of Latin-American thought. Cambridge, Mass., Harvard University Press. 1944. p182-9.

Mariátegui, José Carlos. Notas de Manuel Moreno Sánchez. (Pensadores de América serie no.2) Mexico, D.F., Imprenta Universitaria. 1937. 133p.

Francisco Indalecio Madero (1873-1913)

Apostle of Democracy

Francisco I. Madero, leader of the Mexican Revolution in 1910, was a revolutionist in spite of himself. Although he was the leader of the greatest popular armed uprising that Mexico, or perhaps any country of the Western Hemisphere has seen, his greatness does not lie in that fact. It lies in the remarkable plan he conceived and executed for achieving democracy in Mexico on the basis of the stability developed under the Porfirio Díaz dictatorship. It lies in his political redemption of the Mexican people, and in the political tradition he established.

Refusing to support schemes for armed uprising like those of the Magón brothers, he would have accepted the reelection of Díaz in 1910 if the free election of vice president, congress, governors and state legislatures had been guaranteed. He was convinced that the Mexican people were capable of governing themselves democratically and never faltered in that faith.

Madero believed his real task was the political redemption of a people, and in his fervor and enthusiasm became really a prophet or apostle of the democratic faith, renewing that faith in the hearts of hundreds of thousands of Mexicans long disillusioned by years of revolution and dictatorship. He staked his life on this faith in 1910 when persecution by Díaz officials showed clearly that the promised free election was to be a fraud. It was for the education of his countrymen that he insisted upon exhausting every possibility of constitutional and legal action in the face of persecution, although he realized well that the Díaz regime used the constitution as a subterfuge for its own peculiar politics of force and violence.

Even when arrested a few weeks before the election, Madero refused to allow himself or his party to be tempted to acts of violence. From his prison he continued to direct a remarkable and peaceful demonstration of how organized public opinion could protest against the usurpation of power by a tyranny knowing no law but intrigue and violence. His influence over his political party was so great that his followers continued the campaign, turning out to the polls in astonishing numbers, even when they knew they would be subjected to acts of violence, and that there was not the slightest chance of the government permitting a free election.

Only when the Díaz Congress refused to consider the petition of protest circulated secretly and signed by more than a hundred thousand of his followers, and when the government, thoroughly frightened, ordered his rearrest—only then did Madero raise the standard of revolt. How effective he had been in arousing the nation was shown by the rapidity with which the Díaz regime crumbled before the onslaught of his followers.

Madero came from one of the richest and strongest families of northern Mexico. His grandfather had been governor of Coahuila. His father was a pioneer in developing large scale cotton production by irrigation in the Nazas valley in Coahuila and Durango, now the center of Mexico's greatest experiment in agricultural cooperatives.

He was born October 30, 1873, on the hacienda El Rosario near Parras, Coahuila. Early education at home was followed by study in a Jesuit school at Saltillo. He studied also in St. Mary's College, Baltimore, in several schools in France, and in the University of California. Returning home, he was given a large estate in the Nazas valley by his father. He managed his estate well and took a sympathetic interest in the health, education and welfare of his workers. He married and prospered. His chief interest seemed to be his estate and a proposal for a dam to control the annual floods of the Nazas River, upon which irrigation of the valley depended.

But the political situation in 1909-10 brought his great opportunity. Already he had been instrumental in organizing a political party in Coahuila which refused to play Porfirista politics and sought to restore self-rule there. When General Díaz, aware that he probably had only a few more years to live, announced that the presidential election in 1910 would be free, Madero and his friends at once made plans to extend their organization on a national scale. His book, *The Presidential Succession in 1910*, published on the eve of the campaign, was the spark which set off the flame. Although written in carefully measured language to avoid personal offense to Díaz, this book was a frank and devastating condemnation of the Díaz system, and a clarion call to the Mexican people to assert their constitutional democratic rights. It was so well written, in fact, that his grandfather refused to believe that Francisco had written it.

Madero was convinced that stable, democratic government was a necessary prelude to any program of social advance. Although well aware of Mexico's social and economic problems, he proposed social reforms much less radical than those which have since followed. During his campaign he promised industrial workers complete respect for their right to organize, and workmen's compensation and other laws which would "better the situation of the worker." He also promised restoration of lands wrongfully taken from Indian communities, federal aid for a program of general education, termination of the system of monopolistic concessions, and colonization of public lands by small, rather than large landholders.

Madero's overthrow in 1913 was due to army intrigues with reactionary elements, unfortunately, with apparent encouragement from the United States official representative. It was due, also, to the very strength of the elements of rebellion he had loosed, to his failure to consolidate his political position, and to his weakness in trusting men like Victoriano Huerta. He was imprisoned and murdered. His great reform movement degenerated into seven years of vicious civil war. But Madero did not fail; he became a martyr. The real failure was the failure of Díaz to take advantage of the essentially sound plan of redemption Madero proposed. For Madero's plan was not really one of revolution. The revolutionary Plan of San Luis Potosí, which he was forced to issue in late 1910, was an improvisation. In the bitter years of the civil war, and since, Mexico had to begin again to learn the lesson of democracy Madero tried to teach.

Madero, Francisco I. La sucesión presidencial en 1910. Mexico, Librería de Educación de B. de la Prida. 1909. 308p.

O'Shaughnessey, Edith Louise. Intimate pages of Mexican history. New York, George H. Doran. 1920. p147-88.

Taracena, Alfonso. Francisco I. Madero. Mexico, Botas. 1937. 604p.

Venustiano Carranza (1859-1920)

First Chief of the Mexican Revolution

For seven years, from 1913 to 1920, the tall, patriarchal and bespectacled figure of Venustiano Carranza towered over other leaders in the Mexican Revolution. That maelstrom of civil and military conflict, that strange composite of idealism and petty greed, of statesmanship and partisan politics, which Mexicans call the Revolution, forced many men from obscurity into positions of sudden and unexpected responsibility. But none so completely personified all the tendencies of the Revolution, good and bad, false and true, none dominated the scene, towering above others in time of crisis, as did Carranza. He was not a man of great vision, perhaps, not a great idealistic leader. But although his views may have been limited, he was a rugged character, a man of indomitable courage and will. Almost by sheer personal force he continued to give unity and purpose to the revolutionary movement in the midst of the anarchy which followed Madero's death.

He is a controversial figure, and contradictory in many respects. To the loyal Coahuilans who followed him from his first defiance of the usurping Huerta in 1913 to the end of his life, he represented the moral integrity and the spirit of honest, patriotic purpose which brought the revolutionary cause safely through its many attempted betrayals by less farsighted, or less persevering leaders. Yet his name became the basis of a new word "carrancear" used by the sharp tongues of Mexico City to describe the self-seeking of Revolutionary generals. Some writers, particularly in the United States, have represented him as a social radical, others as a reactionary. By some Mexicans he is accused of traitorous plotting with the gringoes, while by others he is held up as the heroic protector of his country against Yankee intervention. He has been called atheistic, and defended as a friend of Christianity and the Church. Even among serious Mexican students of the Revolution today, his career is the source of the most violent dispute.

This air of controversy surrounding the figure of the great "First Chief of the Revolution" makes it difficult to arrive at a balanced view of his role in Mexican affairs. Yet Carranza was not a complicated personality. With due allowance for human frailty and errors he was representative of the best of the traditional liberal leadership which had persisted in Mexico through nearly a century of defeat and frustration. He was the transition between the old liberalism and the new, twentieth century spirit of reform. His stubborn devotion to the old liberalism was really the source of his ability to give the Revolution organization and stability where others failed.

Venustiano Carranza was born December 29, 1859, in the town of Cuatro Ciénegas, in the state of Coahuila. His father, Jesús Carranza, had been a friend and loyal supporter of Benito Juárez, and a man of prominence in his state, although he took no large part in national politics. For Venustiano as for his father the ideal of Juárez was a powerful example. The Carranza clan were large landholders in Coahuila, and were respected as strong men, obstinate in any purpose to which they set themselves. From his father Venustiano inherited the commanding physique and determination of the Carranzas, and from his mother, María Garza, a more kindly, affable temperament, probably the source of much of the great personal loyalty and attachment which his many followers had for him.

Carranza's education was good but not extensive. As a boy he attended the Jesuit school in Saltillo. From there he went to the National Preparatory School in Mexico City, until a serious eye ailment forced him to withdraw. The eye difficulty was afterward cured by an oculist in the United States, but Carranza, instead of returning to his studies, went back to Cuatro Ciénegas. Here he married Virginia Salinas, and settled down to a life of cattle raising and farming.

At the age of twenty-seven he took his first step in politics, and was elected municipal president of his home town. As municipal president he clashed with the governor of Coahuila, Garza Galán, and was forced to give up his office and retire to private life. Then in 1893, with his brother Emilio and a few friends, he organized a successful uprising which prevented the re-election of the governor. He became a partisan of General Bernardo Reyes, the great Monterey caudillo of liberal tendencies who continued to oppose the Díaz regime until 1910. To him Carranza probably owed his membership in the national senate.

Yet, while Carranza became a Reyista, he was never Reyes' man in the sense that he sacrificed his own independence. This appeared in 1909 when he became the candidate for governor of the state of Coahuila. Although Reyes chose the easy way out at this time by accepting a diplomatic mission to Europe, Carranza persisted in his candidacy, even when the party of *científicos* persuaded President Díaz to order him to withdraw. He encouraged Madero's presidential plans in 1910, and when the Madero revolt broke out in January 1911, went to San Antonio to join the movement. As a result Madero made him chief of military operations in the region of Coahuila, Tamaulipas and Nuevo León.

Carranza was the only member of Madero's intimate circle to oppose the agreement made at Ciudad Juárez in which Díaz agreed to withdraw in favor of a provisional president. Carranza opposed, insisting that there was no hope of inaugurating a new order in Mexico until there had been a decisive defeat of the military forces upon which the Díaz system depended. Events, unfortunately, proved he was right.

His real test and his real opportunity came in 1913 when Victoriano Huerta, by a *coup d'etat,* made himself dictator. Carranza, as governor of Coahuila, refused to recognize the assassin of President Madero as president, and began the military resistance which eventually brought Huerta's overthrow. Defeating Huerta he disbanded the federal army, thus avoiding a repetition of the fatal mistake of 1911.

But the military leaders failed to agree upon the establishment of a government in the convention which followed, and in the chaos and civil war which ensued Carranza faced an even more serious situation than had Madero before. Villa, Zapata and Obregón were the great popular leaders, although a large number of others of less prominence also played important roles. Villa was defeated by Obregón in the Battle of Celaya, and Zapata, the agrarian leader, was soon eliminated by assassination. Carranza was not personally responsible for Zapata's assassination, but it is one of the greatest blots on his administration, nevertheless. Opposition did not end with the elimination of Villa and Zapata, but Carranza was now able to consolidate his regime by securing his election as constitutional president and by a series of reform measures incorporated in the constitution drawn up at Querétaro in 1917.

Carranza himself was inclined toward moderate rather than radical social and political views. His concept of the reforms required in Mexico, like that of Madero, was largely political. However, the agrarian movement, fired by Zapata's magic name and by the workers movement, and supported by groups in Orizaba, Mexico City, Puebla and elsewhere, had become too strong to be ignored. Moreover, there was now an insistent demand for regulation of the giant petroleum industry, a demand which grew in part out of the fact that the boom in petroleum coincided with the most disorderly period of the revolution, and in part out of the anti-Yankee feeling engendered by the occupation of Vera Cruz (1914) and the Pershing Punitive Expedition. Carranza issued decrees dealing with land and petroleum in 1915, but the definitive statements of these, as on labor and related matters, came in the new constitution. Now famous, especially among sister republics which have taken its provisions as models, the new constitution went far toward the nationalization of natural resources, provided for an advanced code of social legislation, especially in labor matters, provided for the distribution of land among the landless peons, and adopted a revolutionary program of popular education. It is the outstanding event of Carranza's regime.

Continued disorder and opposition throughout his presidency made it impossible for Carranza to carry out these reforms to any great extent. In fact, such success as he enjoyed was due in considerable measure to one fact quite unrelated to the reform program. It was the rapidly expanding national income from taxes on petroleum, production of which was skyrocketing because of the First World War. Petroleum taxes provided the funds needed to keep rebellious generals in line. Control of the generals, in turn, made it possibly gradually to consolidate the reforms of the constitution by building a military force to replace the disbanded Federals.

Relations with the United States were a source of constant difficulty. Woodrow Wilson helped Carranza to power, yet Carranza found himself forced by Mexican nationalism, if not inclined by his own views, to a policy of obstructionism against the United States. Publication of the Zimmerman note, indeed, made it look as if Carranza had been dealing with Germany for sinister purposes. Although the known facts do not entirely warrant this view, there is no doubt of his hostility to the United States at the time. He was not strong enough to prevent the Pershing Punitive Expedition, yet he did everything in his power to prevent its success. But he was first and foremost a Mexican nationalist, and too taken up with Mexico's internal problem to become involved in a quixotic plan such as the Zimmerman note suggested, to recover Mexico's irredenta.

Carranza's overthrow in the Revolution of 1920 had neither radical nor conservative meaning. Carranza simply made the mistake of blocking the candidacy of the popular Álvaro Obregón, and backing the unpopular Ignacio Bonillas. Disgruntled labor groups joined forces with conservatives or reactionaries, and with opportunistic guerrilla chiefs like General Pelaez of Vera Cruz in support of the uprising led by Obregón, Adolfo de la Huerta and Elias Calles, all of Sonora.

Facing inevitable defeat, Carranza, with a small party, tried to escape to Vera Cruz, only to have his train attacked on the way. He escaped instead to the mountains of Puebla. But there in the remote village of Tlaxcalantongo he was treacherously murdered as he slept, by the local guerrilla chieftain who had offered him protection.

Before leaving the National Palace in Mexico City on May 7, 1920, he had remarked, with apparent premonition of the fate in store for him, "Now they will see how a President of the Republic dies." And so it was, for in death the figure of the First Chief assumed greater proportions than at any time during his lifetime. Not all the animosities and hatreds of the civil war died with him at Tlaxcalantongo, but Mexico from that point on entered a new era of stability and steady advance toward the ideals of the Revolution and the Constitution of 1917.

Fornaro, Carlo de. Carranza and Mexico. New York. Kennerley. 1915. 242p. (Chapters by I. C. Enriquez, Charles Ferguson and M. C. Rolland)

Mena Brito, Bernardino. Carranza, sus amigos y sus enemigos. Mexico, Botas. 1935. 698p.

Víctor Raúl Haya de la Torre (1895-   )

Leader of APRA

The term Indo-America has come into common use to designate the large area of America, extending from northern Mexico south to the northern border of Chile, and including northwestern Argentina, where the population is predominantly Indian and mestizo. Within this area, in Mexico and Peru, are found the two most surprising and outstanding liberal movements in Latin America today.

In Peru the movement centers around the APRA (Popular Alliance for American Revolution), a political party originating in groups of student workers which for more than a decade has agitated for land and labor reform, the building of schools, and regeneration of the Indian. Its leadership is part of the new political generation in Latin America, a generation which is determined to establish political and social democracy. APRA has not succeeded in capturing political control of the country, perhaps never will. But its influence has been great.

The political genius who organized it, and who has presided over its destinies, is Víctor Raúl Haya de la Torre. His is a name of magic for the disinherited of Peru, a name which appears mysteriously, painted at night in huge letters on the Peruvian mountain sides. It is on the lips of workers in city factories and the huge plantations of the coastal rivers. For to thousands of Peruvians this leader of the youth of Latin America has become the incarnation of a great social movement in a way and to an extent rarely achieved by a political leader.

Haya de la Torre was born in Trujillo, Peru, February 22, 1895, in the midst of troubled times and civil disorder. The revolution of 1895 brought the overthrow of the dictator-president, Cáceres, and his German trained army. Guerrilla forces (montoneros), supported by the Civilista party composed of rich landowners like the Pardos and Leguías, joined with the great democratic leader Piérola to bring about Cáceres' downfall. Víctor Raúl's father, Raúl Edmundo Haya, was a journalist of liberal tendencies. His mother, Zoila Victoria de la Torre y Cárdenas, was descended from one of the old colonial and landowning families, but had little wealth of her own.

In 1910 Raúl Edmundo lost his small fortune, and his family faced poverty. The next seven years were years of hard work yet of growth in many ways for young Víctor Raúl. He taught school for a while to help pay his expenses in the University of La Libertad in Trujillo. He helped his father publish a paper, *La Industria*. In partnership with his brother, he organized the first athletic club in Trujillo, the Club Jorge Chávez, named for the adventurous mountain climber whose exploits were then being acclaimed. Because he was discontented with the "colonialism" of the university, he organized the students into a University Center where social and political questions of the day could be discussed. Of special interest in those days were the conflicts of the popular President Billinghurst with his recalcitrant congress.

In 1917 Haya went to Lima to the University of San Marcos. Here he at once began to take an active part in the work of the Student Federation. The following year he was elected president of the Federation, and in 1919 led the students in a strike against reactionary policies of university authorities which forbade study or teaching of current problems. José Matías Manzanilla became interested in the young student at this time and engaged him to assist in drafting a project for a revision of labor and social laws.

But Haya de la Torre soon became disgusted with Manzanilla's "reforms" which changed nothing. One day he went to the National Library to make the acquaintance of the great liberal, Manuel González Prada. González Prada by this time was an old man. Although he had spent a lifetime in apparently fruitless fighting for the liberal cause in Peru he still was not disillusioned. He died about a year after Haya's first meeting with him, but that year was sufficient for him to exert a great influence over his young friend and to convince him that his life, too, should be devoted to the cause of reform.

When the University of San Marcos was closed by the Leguía dictatorship in 1919 because of student agitation, Haya de la Torre went to the University of Cuzco, where he organized the first National Student Conference in 1920. In 1921 he was president of the International Students' Conference of Montevideo. Back in Lima he founded a peoples' university which he named Manuel González Prada, to further education especially among the working class. The university was staffed chiefly by students from the schools of law and medicine. He urged close cooperation of student leaders with the working class, and in 1923 led a group of students and workers in a large anti-clerical demonstration. When police fired on the demonstrators a student and a workingman were killed. Haya de la Torre's eloquent address at the funeral of the victims brought his deportation.

José Vasconcelos, the Mexican secretary of education and an ardent patron of the youth movement, invited him to Mexico. During the months which followed he was honored by invitations to the universities of Mexico, Argentina, Chile, Cuba and Panama. In Argentina he was welcomed by José Ingenieros, great Argentine liberal professor of the University at

Buenos Aires, and author of *Mediocre Man* and other books widely read by the students of Latin America. In Cuba Haya de la Torre founded the popular university named for the Cuban liberator, José Martí, and encouraged student organizations and workers in their opposition to the Machado distatorship. In England he lived and studied at Oxford and Cambridge. He also visited Russia and Italy studying conditions there. In cooperation with the Argentine anti-imperialist, Manuel Ugarte, he established a center of Latin American studies in Paris.

After the overthrow of Leguía he was called back to Peru by the APRA to be their candidate for the presidency in opposition to the military leader of the revolt, Colonel Sánchez Cerro. The campaign produced bloody clashes of Apristas with the military, especially in Trujillo. Haya de la Torre was viciously persecuted, imprisoned, and held incommunicado by Sánchez Cerro for sixteen months in 1932-33, in spite of the intervention of Upton Sinclair, Sinclair Lewis, Romain Rolland, George Lansbury, Ortega y Gassett, Miguel Unamuno and many others. Sánchez Cerro was assassinated by a university student and an amnesty law of the succeeding Benavides administration at last brought freedom to Haya. In a huge arena of Lima a crowd of 50,000 persons hailed his release. How much had been accomplished was further shown in the social provisions of the new constitution of 1933 which were really a victory for APRA. The influence of APRA is further apparent in the social program of the present administration.

The APRA has always argued that foreign imperialism was largely responsible for dictatorship and reactionary social policies in Latin America. Even as late as 1938 Haya de la Torre attacked the Lima Conference in a book, *The Eighth Pan American Conference: Another Farce?* But the war in Europe has brought many changes. In 1940 he dramatically indicated the end of his anti-Yankee agitation and acceptance of the United States democratic leadership by telegraphing congratulations to President Roosevelt on his reelection.

This was a major triumph for the Good Neighbor Policy in Latin America.

Cossío del Pomar, Filipe. Haya de la Torre, el Indoamericano. Mexico, Editorial América. 1939. 291p.

Foreign Affairs. 13:236-46. January 1935. Aprismo; the rise of Haya de la Torre. Carleton Beals.

Haya de la Torre, Raúl. El antimperialismo y el Apra. Santiago de Chile, Ercilla. 1936. 192p.

Haya de la Torre, Raúle. ¿A donde va Indoamérica? 2nd ed. Santiago de Chile, Ercilla. 1935. 280p.

Haya de la Torre, Raúl. El plan del aprismo. Lima, Editorial Libertad. 1933. 70p.

Haya de la Torre, Raúl. Por la emancipación de América latina, artículos, mensajes, discursos, 1923-1927. Buenos Aires, M. Gleizer. 1927. 212p.

Hispanic American Historical Review. 23:555-85. August 1943. Aprista bibliography. Luis Alberto Sánchez.

Sánchez, Luis Alberto. Raúl Haya de la Torre, o el político. Santiago de Chile, Ercilla. 1934. 237p.

Who's Who in Latin America. P. A. Martin, ed. 1940.

José Vasconcelos (1882-   )

Creole Ulysses

Anyone even casually acquainted with the recent history of Latin America knows of Vasconcelos as the Mexican Secretary of Education in whose great energy and contagious enthusiasm originated the ambitious Mexican school program—the greatest educational movement of this century in the Western Hemisphere. But only those who have studied the history of the Mexican Revolution and the intellectual and cultural trends of Latin America during the last few decades are aware of the great role his philosophical and critical intelligence has played, not only in Mexico, but in the culture and thought of all Latin America.

His more than twenty-five published volumes, his numerous contributions to magazines and newspapers, and the journals which he edited, constitute one of the richest sources for the intellectual and cultural movements of Latin America during the last quarter century. With proper allowance for the prejudice of the author, they are an invaluable source, also, for the history of the Mexican Revolution. For this successful lawyer and scholar, who gave up a profitable law practice to follow the fortunes of Madero, became the center of some of the bitterest Mexican political conflicts. In the loneliness of years of exile, obliged sometimes to earn a meagre living by hack-writing, he became so disillusioned and pessimistic because of the prostitution of the ideals for which he had fought, that he seemed sometimes to have lost his reason completely. The greatest intellectual figure cast up by the Revolution, he was complicated, paradoxical, contradictory, a dynamic crusader. For years he was the pride of the Mexican nation. Yet in later years he turned almost, if not entirely, reactionary. He repudiated many of his earlier liberal ideas for a medieval, mystic colonialism. Perhaps he is the Revolution's greatest spiritual tragedy.

He has been called the tempestuous, volcanic Vasconcelos, and he has called himself, aptly, the Creole Ulysses. His autobiography in four large volumes was a sensational best-seller in Mexico when is appeared. It has been called the frankest autobiography since Rousseau. It is so vitriolic that some of the targets of his tempestuous and corrosive outbursts of criticism have called him a madman and his charges the lies of a disordered intelligence.

Perhaps Vasconcelos' genius is a kind of madness. But his educational crusade during the days of the Obregón presidency, a crusade which burst from the ministry of education under his direction with the irresistible fury of a volcanic eruption, will never be forgotten. Nor will it be forgotten that he was one of the great inspirations of the new political generation in Mexico and throughout Latin America. For years he wandered an exile in Europe, South America and the United States, pondering his nation's ills and searching for their meaning. He dreamed of a "cosmic race" in America; he was all but consumed by his obsession of Yankee-phobia; always he was the restless, divinely discontented spirit of the Homeric epic, driven to desperation by the punishments the gods were visiting on him, presumably in accordance with some plan of divine vengeance on his un-happy Mexico.

Vasconcelos was born in Oaxaca, February 28, 1882. While his father was a customs agent in Piedras Negras he attended the public school across the border in Eagle Pass, Texas. Later he studied in Yucatan, when his father was transferred there, and in the University of Mexico. He com-pleted the legal course at the University in 1915, and soon established a lucrative law practice in Mexico City. His real talent, however, became evident in the Atheneum of Youth, a literary philosophical club of which he was a founder and a leading spirit. The Atheneum gathered together a brilliant group of young men: the philosopher Antonio Caso, the architect Jesús Acevedo, the painter Diego Rivera and others. Far from limiting themselves to literary and cultural topics, this group of future revolutionary leaders boldly launched forth in discussions of the social and political prob-lems of Mexico. They were seeking a philosophical and cultural basis for its regeneration.

The Madero revolution caught them all up. Vasconcelos joined the Madero Anti-reelectionist Club and edited a paper for the Madero cause. When the paper was suppressed and Madero arrested by the frightened Díaz regime, Vasconcelos succeeded in escaping to the United States. There he represented the Madero movement in Washington, living in a cheap boarding house, where he spent two or three dollars a week of his own money for rent. After the triumph of Madero he became rector of the reorganized National University.

It was under the Obregón presidency, as Secretary of Education from 1921 to 1923, that he did his greatest work. He inspired nine hundred young Mexican men and women to go out with the zeal of the old Spanish missionaries into the Indian villages in an unprecedented educational and cultural crusade. He initiated a cheap popular press in the ministry of education, he introduced new and vigorous young spirits like Lombardo Toledano and others into the National University, and encouraged the de-velopment of the Mexican school of mural painters by putting Rivera and other young artists to work on schools and on the new Education Building. Representatives of the rising political and intellectual generation in Latin

America such as Haya de la Torre, the Chilean poet Gabriela Mistral, and the Nicaraguan rebel poet de la Selva, were brought to Mexico to make it the greatest center of restless, idealistic spirits in the hemisphere. And over all Vasconcelos was the great presiding figure, infusing all with his contagious enthusiasm.

But he quarrelled with Obregón and Calles over their military system and went into exile again. This time he traversed in triumph the lecture halls of universities in France, the United States and Latin America. When Calles announced a free election in 1930, Vasconcelos returned to campaign for the presidency. The outburst of public opinion and resentment against the repressive and exploitive features of the political group brought out by his campaign, was the most tempestuous which Mexico had seen since the Madero campaign of 1910. The election was obviously controlled, and the bitterness of his defeat seared Vasconcelos' spirit. From his exile in the United States he poured out violent and unmeasured invective. The spirit of Ulysses was at last crushed in anguish.

There followed years of lonely suffering and despair. During the last years of the Cárdenas administration he returned to Mexico. Today he is properly rewarded by a long-ungrateful nation with the post of Director of the National Library. With the spirit of "joyful pessimism" of which he wrote in 1930, he is turning some of his former tempestuous energy to the construction of a new building for the library, combining the byzantine-like style of the old colonial churches with a structure suited to modern library needs. But when the writer, with obvious reference to the magnificent Education Building of eighteen years ago, suggested that now Mexico would have two memorials to his work, he replied, "I also built a few schools."

Carrión, Benjamín. Los creadores de la nueva América. Madrid, Sociedad General Española de Librería. 1928. p23-76.

Crawford, W. Rex. A century of Latin-American thought. Cambridge, Mass., Harvard University Press. 1944. p260-76.

Villaseñor y Sánchez, José. El sistema filosófico de Vasconcelos; esayo de crítica filosófica. Mexico, Editorial Polis. 1939.

Vasconcelos, José. Autobiography: Ulises Criollo; La tormenta; El desastre; El proconsulado. Mexico, Botas. 1935-1939. 4v.

Vasconcelos, José. Serie Pensamiento de América, No. 1. Mexico, Secretaría de Educación. 1942. 229p. Prologo de Genaro Fernando MacGregor.

Who's Who in Latin America. P. A. Martin, ed. 1940.

Pedro Aguirre Cerda (1879-1941)

Organizer of Chilean Popular Front

The election of 1938 in Chile was an epoch-marking event in the history of democracy in America. The Popular Front, a coalition of the Radical, Democratic, Socialist and Communist parties with the support of the Chilean Confederation of Workers (CTCH) nominated and elected as president the candidate of the middle class Radical Party, Pedro Aguirre Cerda. It was surprising but understandable for a prosperous lawyer, landowner, and educational pioneer, with a brilliant record of successful participation in politics, a steady adherent to the middle class Radical Party in spite of his eligible social position, to be elected to take the place of the great liberal Arturo Alessandri, with whom he had gone into political exile during the days of the military dictatorship of Ibáñez. But for this man to be elected with the solid support of all the left wing parties, including the Communists, was an indication of how far Chile has gone in recent years in social democracy.

Pedro Aguirre Cerda was born in 1879 in Pocuro, near Los Andes, in the midst of the mountains of central Chile, in the region where the great Argentine liberal Sarmiento spent long years of exile. His parents were poor but independent farmers. He attended the little rural school of his village, the Liceo of San Felipe and the National University in Santiago, where he studied education and law. His father's early death made it necessary for him to begin teaching before finishing his course at the university, and he taught in several schools including the historic National Institute. Without discontinuing his teaching he began to practice law. At night he taught special classes for workers. His brilliant success in these fields brought him in 1910 a government commission for two years of study of administrative law and finance in the Sorbonne.

On his return to Chile he became an active member of the Radical Party of Arturo Alessandri. In 1915 he was elected deputy to Congress from Los Andes, and in 1918 from Santiago. That same year he was appointed Minister of Education and Justice, but after serving only a year was sent to Washington as Financial Counselor of the Chilean Embassy. While in the United States he became greatly interested in the new systems of industrial education then developing.

In 1920 Arturo Alessandri was elected president in a great popular campaign, and he recalled Aguirre Cerda from Washington to organize his cabinet under the parliamentary-cabinet system of government then in use in Chile. The forty-year-old teacher-lawyer was thus thrust into the very center of Alessandri's desperate struggle to enact a program of labor laws and social legislation against the opposition of the landowning oligarchy intrenched in the Congress. In the crisis provoked by the constitutional reforms of 1925, the Minister of War, Ibáñez, supported by the army, headed a conservative revolt and established himself as a military dictator. Aguirre Cerda went into exile with Alessandri.

During a five-year exile in Paris he published two books which gave great additional impetus to the reform movement in Chile, *The Industrial Problem*, and *The Agrarian Problem*. On his return after the overthrow of Ibáñez in 1930, he found Chile in the midst of the most severe economic crisis experienced by any American state in the great debacle following 1929. Complete collapse of the nitrate industry had taken away the government's largest single source of income. Unemployment and economic distress were widespread, and national bankruptcy threatened. In the midst of this chaos Aguirre Cerda tranquilly pursued his duties as Professor of Political Economy in the University of Chile, and tried out his industrial theories as manager of the National Industrial Shops established by the government to teach men and women the skills of small home industries. In 1934 he established the School of Industry and Commerce in the University and became its first dean. He made his estancia, "Conchale," a model of its kind, paying better wages than the Chilean law required, giving profit-sharing bonuses, and free vacations at the seaside to his employees.

Gradually he drifted away from Alessandri, who was elected president again in 1932 with the support of the old Liberal and Conservative Parties. Economic conditions continued desperate in Chile, while the rest of the world moved slowly away from the brink of the economic vortex of 1930. The exigencies of the financial position drove the government increasingly toward policies of retrenchment, and made it look with disfavor on any proposal for social or economic reform in the interest of wage earners. Reform elements became more and more desperate. Aguirre Cerda conceived the brilliant political plan of capturing and canalizing this radical discontent into a constructive program under the leadership of the middle class Radical Party. The Popular Front, made possible by the withdrawal of Marmaduke Grove, Socialist candidate and head of the leftist government of 1932, was the result.

In office Aguirre Cerda was patient, willing to effect changes slowly. All his patience was needed, for a disastrous earthquake in January 1939, required postponement of all plans of reform for the time being. The situation following the earthquake was handled efficiently however. Organization of labor unions increased and new legislation extended the benefits of social and health insurance. Contrary to expectation in some quarters, there was no persecution of foreign capital. In the Congress opposition was still great to certain agrarian projects such as organization of rural workers, minimum wages for farm laborers, and land reform. Meanwhile new elementary schools were established in a determined drive to eliminate illiteracy, with the old motto of Sarmiento, "To govern is to educate." The Second World War also helped to consolidate Aguirre's political situation by bringing together all the liberal elements of the country in opposition to pro-fascist tendencies represented by such groups as the since-outlawed Popular Socialist Vanguard of Jorge González von Mares.

In the midst of all this activity, Aguirre Cerda's sudden and unexpected death in 1941 came as one of the most serious blows to democratic reform experienced recently anywhere in the western hemisphere.

Bulletin of the Pan American Union. 73:1-2. January 1939. New president of Chile.

Current Biography. H. W. Wilson Co. 1941. p12-14.

Nation. 148:62-4. January 14, 1939. Democracy wins in Chile. Freda Kirchwey.

New York Times. November 26, 1941.

Nuevo Orden. No. 1, p. 7-10. October 1940. Don Pedro Aguirre Cerda y el frente popular de Chile. (Published in Mexico, D. F.)

Who's Who in Latin America. P. A. Martin, ed. 1940.

Manuel Prado Ugarteche (1889-   )

Liberal Conservative

Manuel Prado Ugarteche, president of Peru since 1939, although further to the right than most of the new generation of political leaders in Latin America, is, nevertheless, a good example of that new generation. Both a liberal and a conservative, he typifies in many ways the conjunction of forces which are today producing a remarkable awakening in Peru, so long steeped in colonialism. Through both his father and his mother he is descended from landowning families of Huánaco and Arequipa noted for devotion to arms and politics, which have always played prominent roles in Peruvian history. His father was twice president of Peru, and a considerably older brother was a hero of the Cuban Ten Years War for independence, and a hero-martyr in the War of the Pacific against Chile.

President Prado is a distinguished mathematician and scientist, the author of books on hydrostatics and meteorology, a former professor of higher mathematics in the oldest university in America, San Marcos, and a former editor of a scientific journal. He has been president of a steamship company, and for five years was president of a bank. His record as a liberal is impressive. During his student days he took an active part in Peruvian and international student congresses. In 1912, as an election official he showed great bravery in keeping the election polls under his charge open in the face of great disturbances.

As a member of Congress, during the Leguía administration, he bravely opposed various financial plans of the dictator, urged plans of social assistance and public health, and became the leader of the opposition, a leadership which cost him eleven years of political exile (1921-32). His family connections in the ruling class, and in the traditional political parties, his academic career, and his broad business and financial experience have been great assets in the far reaching program he has inaugurated as president. But the most significant thing about his presidency is that as a member of the privileged class he personally represents the realization of that class in Peru that the great movement of social protest, of which the APRA has been the mouthpiece, must be satisfied.

Manuel Prado was born in Lima, April 21, 1889, the son of ex-president General Mariano Ignacio Prado and Magdalena Ugarteche de Prado. Educated in Jesuit secondary schools in Lima and Paris, he received his professional training in the School of Engineering in Lima and in the University of San Marcos. He represented the students of Peru in the first International

Conference of Students in Montevideo in 1907, and was to have been a representative in the second conference at Buenos Aires in 1910, but was prevented from attending by the outbreak of a border dispute with Ecuador in that year. Instead he made a vigorous campaign of fiery speeches, and enlisted in the army which was being gathered to repel invasion. Fortunately the invasion which was feared, did not occur. In 1914 he received the military rank of lieutenant for fighting side by side with Colonel (later president) Benavides in the Revolution of that year.

From 1915 until the closing of the university by President Leguía in 1919, he was professor of higher mathematics in the Faculty of Science of the University of San Marcos. During those years he also edited the *Revista de Ciencias* published by the University. In 1910 he was elected to Congress from the province of Huamachuco, scene of the last desperate Peruvian resistance in the war against Chile, and where his older brother Leoncio met his death in that war. The opposition in Congress, of which Prado soon became the leader, had little direct connection with the gathering storm of social protest represented in the APRA. It represented rather the socially conscious elements of the dominant social and political class who saw the importance of protest, and felt that the Leguía administration by its suppression of liberty and its extravagant program of public works, many of them of doubtful social and economic value, was aggravating rather than improving the situation.

Prado's opposition soon brought political exile. Like Aguirre Cerda of Chile, he spent much of his time during his years of exile in study and discussion of the social and economic ills of his country. When he returned in 1932, after the Sánchez Cerro revolution, it was with fully matured social ideas for the development of his country, ideas in which popular education figured largely. For two years he was president of the Companía Peruana de Vapores. In 1934, under the administration of his old friend President Benavides, he became president of the politically important Central Reserve Bank where he remained until his election to the presidency.

In his message to Congress on July 28, 1941, President Prado said, "Peru has one of the most advanced programs of social legislation in America. No other country of the continent surpasses it in the realization of the postulates of authentic social justice." One of his chief interests, he said, is hygienic housing. This is reflected in government housing projects for workers in Lima and elsewhere. His government has encouraged the formation of workers' and farmers' cooperatives. The public restaurants and the program of free meals and other special services to children and pregnant mothers, offered under the National Children's Institute, and the program of social insurance and medical services have been improved and extended. A determined campaign to improve public health includes compulsory vaccination and an intensive effort to reduce the amount of malaria.

The right of workers to organize and engage in the activities of their organizations is apparently recognized fully. In the same message to Congress President Prado stated confidently that he felt the organized workers were supporting the program of social legislation. True to his scientific background, he has encouraged a wide program of statistical studies of social and economic conditions as the basis for further legislation. A concordat has settled the question of church-state relations for the first time in nearly a century, and the church is supporting the new social program.

But the best evidence of seriousness of purpose in Prado's administration is the school program and new school law of April 1, 1941. Even before this law, three hundred and fifty schools with seven hundred and forty teachers were established in 1940. Four new normal schools modeled after those of Mexico have since been established to train rural teachers. The university, the center of so much agitation and discontent in recent years, has been democratized in various ways, and a Commission of Education has been created to direct a great national educational program. It now remains to be seen whether the school program will be continued and accelerated as it must be if the high illiteracy rate of about 60 per cent is to be overcome. But, all in all, President Prado's six-year term gives promise of having educational significance comparable to that of Cárdenas in Mexico.

Gunther, John. Inside Latin America. New York, Harper & Brothers. 1941. p203-5.

Prado Ugarteche, Manuel. Presidential message to congress, July 28, 1941. (Published by the Peruvian government).

Who's Who in Latin America. P. A. Martin, ed. 1940.

Christian Science Monitor. December 1, 1939.

Current Biography. H. W. Wilson Co. 1942. p676-9.

LÁZARO CÁRDENAS (1895-   )

Fulfillment of the Mexican Revolution

It is perhaps an indication of the deep social significance of the Mexican Revolution that in three decades it has not produced a really dominant figure. Great figures, yes, but not one person who can be singled out as the personification of the movement. Francisco Madero, its first leader, loosed forces greater than he imagined existed and found himself carried away by a whirlwind which he was unable to guide or control. Emiliano Zapata personified the deep dissatisfaction of the landless masses, but lacked a sense of the broader social and political implications of the movement. Francisco Villa, the most colorful leader, represented strong forces of social discontent, but in the final analysis he was simply the super-caudillo, the demagogic strong man characteristic of the political and social disorder of Latin America. The great intellectual, Vasconcelos, failed in his effort to achieve greatness as a political leader.

Álvaro Obregón was probably the greatest military commander, although not the greatest military intelligence of the Revolution. He personifies the triumph of the spirit of order and obedience over lawlessness; he was the only man who could defeat Villa. Obregón came near greatness as president. Because of the great freedom he gave to his ministers, notably his minister of education, José Vasconcelos, Mexico became the mecca of the new reforming generation of Latin Americans. But Obregón seemed to lack a program of his own, and in his fatal effort to secure reelection he showed either cynical disregard or a serious underestimate of the strength of the social movement he headed, an error which greatly retarded its social program for nearly a decade later.

It is Lázaro Cárdenas, president of Mexico 1934-1940, who is in many ways the most representative figure the Revolution has produced. Like the great mass of Mexicans he is a mestizo, of Indian and white blood. He was born May 21, 1895, in Jiquilpán de Juárez, near Uruapan in the state of Michoacán, where the mass of the population is descended wholly or in part from the Tarascan Indians. His career is typical of the self-made political generals of the Revolution. In 1913 he was the youthful proprietor of a printing shop when he joined the Constitutional forces fighting to overthrow the military dictatorship of Victoriano Huerta, the betrayor of Madero. He was a brave and successful soldier, and his rise through the revolutionary ranks was rapid.

In Michoacán he played an important role in the movement which brought Obregón to the presidency in 1920. Always loyal to the established government, he was rewarded with the rank of Brigadier General by Obregón and General of Division by Calles. Out of the troubled political situation produced by the reelection and assassination of Obregón he emerged as a figure of national prominence. He became governor of Michoacán (1928-32), president of the executive committee of the official National Revolutionary Party (1930), Secretary of the Interior (1931), commander of the important military district of Puebla (1932), and Secretary of War and Marine in the critical year 1933, when preparations for the election of the next year were under way.

Cárdenas' military and political record gave him the confidence of the army, yet there was still little in his record to suggest a reforming president. During 1933, however, he gained the confidence and support of the increasingly strong labor and agrarian reform groups within the official party who drew up the party platform as a Six Year Plan to complete the social program of the Revolution during the next administration.

That Cárdenas was no ordinary candidate, however, was proved by his energetic and unprecedented electoral campaign and by the enthusiasm he evoked throughout the country. That he was no ordinary president was shown by his determined and successful execution of the Six Year Plan. Some of his measures aroused great controversy: settlement of the strike in the national railways by turning them over to the workers (they were later taken back by the government); official support of the strike of petroleum workers which precipitated confiscation of the foreign owned oil properties; and confiscation and collectivization of the great cotton plantations in the Laguna area, the henequin enterprise in Yucatán, the rice plantations of Lombardía and Nueva Italia in Michoacán, and of the sugar cane plantations in El Mante.

There were numerous other constructive measures, too, during his administration, such as highway building, and new banking institutions. However, two accomplishments stand out because they synthesize Mexico's remarkable social regeneration: the large scale land distribution and the building of schools for the illiterate rural masses. The Cárdenas administration transformed Mexico into a nation of small landowners and gave schools to practically every rural community. This bold attack upon the fundamental problem of the Revolution has given the Mexican government today a confidence and stability it has never known before. When one adds his remarkable success in diplomacy—for he made Mexico the leading Latin American exponent of continental solidarity in spite of the complications of land and oil expropriations—the sum of Cárdenas' achievements is even more imposing.

He was a popular president. In his travels throughout the country he brought the Revolution and its social program home to millions of Mexicans as no other president had been able to do. Yet one may well ask, was it Cárdenas who did these things? Or was it not something bigger than he— the Mexican Revolution, or the very land of Mexico and its disinherited masses?

Freeman, Joseph; Orozco, Luis Chávez; and Gutman, Enrique. Lázaro Cárdenas visto por tres hombres. Mexico, Masas. 1937. 30p.

Prewett, Virginia. The Americas and tomorrow. New York and Philadelphia, Dutton. 1944. p98-100, 125-7.

Watt, Stewart and Peterson, H. F. Builders of Latin America. New York and London, Harper & Brothers. 1942. p279-92.

Weyl, Nathaniel and Sylvia. The reconquest of Mexico. New York and London. Oxford University Press. 1939. 394p.

Who's Who in Latin America. P. A. Martin, ed. 1940.

Nuevo Orden. No. 5, p. 34-7 January 1941. Speech to the 15th Council of the C.T.M., November 25, 1940. (Published in Mexico, D. F.)

INDEX